RUNNING FOR THE PEOPLE?

How Canadian Elections Favour the Career Politician

REM WESTLAND

polarbear lane editions

All rights reserved. No part of this book may be reproduced, stored in a retrieval system or transmitted, in any form or by any means, without the prior written consent of the publisher or a licence from The Canadian Copyright Licensing Agency (Access Copyright). For a copyright licence, visit www.accesscopyright.ca or call toll free to 1-800-893-5777.

polarbear lane editions
Ottawa, Ontario

Library and Archives Canada Cataloguing in Publication

Westland, R. C. (Remmelt Cornelis), 1948–, author
Running for the people? : how Canadian elections favour the career politician / R.C. Westland.

Issued in print and electronic formats.
ISBN 978-0-9940358-0-6 (pbk.).–ISBN 978-0-9940358-1-3 (ebook)

1. Westland, R. C. (Remmelt Cornelis), 1948– –Political activity.
2. Canada. Parliament–Elections, 2011. 3. Political candidates–Canada.
4. Political campaigns–Canada. 5. Elections–Canada. 6. Politics, Practical–Canada. I. Title.

JL193.W57 2015   324.70971   C2015-900686-4
C2015-900687-2

ISBN 978-0-9940358-0-6 (paperback)
ISBN 978-0-9940358-1-3 (ebook)

Cover design by Peter Cocking

15 16 17 18 19   5 4 3 2 1

At my first public event as designated candidate for the Conservative Party of Canada, in the riding of Ottawa–Vanier, I was exhorted by a member of the electoral district association to "always thank your wife!"

As I stumbled through Canada's electoral process, it was easy to forget how much I owed to the people who helped me get from one test to the other. This book is dedicated to Marie La Forest. She is the one to whom I owe the very most.

Running the gauntlet: *A form of physical punishment where captives run between two rows of soldiers who repeatedly strike them; also, a series of tests endured publicly — sometimes eagerly anticipated — to prove worthiness of acceptance into a prestigious group.*

CONTENTS

	Introduction	1
1.	Down the Rabbit Hole	13
2.	The Test of Privacy	27
3.	The Test of Values	50
4.	The Test of Commitment	70
5.	The Test of Leadership	92
6.	The Test of Endurance	113
7.	The Test of Isolation	134
8.	The Test of Accomplishment	141
9.	Looking Back	168
	Conclusion	195
	Acknowledgments	207
	Appendix	209

INTRODUCTION

A crash course in Canada's electoral process began for me when I submitted my name to run in the May 2011 federal election. I was apprehensive about what was going to happen. To keep hold over an unease that threatened to become overwhelming, I kept a record of the experience. This book is about what happened.

I endured various trials along the way — intellectual, psychological, emotional, and physical, most of them absolute surprises. People tell me I should not have been as surprised as I was. I have long been a student of politics and I am a keen reader of political texts and commentary. Throughout my career I have interacted with policy-makers and elected politicians in the federal and provincial governments. Yet I didn't really have a clue.

Nothing I had read or experienced prepared me for what was to come. There is a psychological and physical distance between the will expressed by an individual when that person stands for election and the will expressed by the electorate on the day of a vote. This distance has been detailed in laws and regulations. It has been described in works of fiction and non-fiction. It has been filmed in blockbuster movies and in documentaries. This book is different. It draws from the daily grind and personal angst of one particular candidate, offers a way to understand what happened, and summarizes the lessons learned. This is the book I wish I could have read before my journey began.

Because this story about one person's run for office is a true story, the people who appear alongside the runner are real. The runner's advisors and handlers, except for one, are alive and well and only four years older now than they were at the time. I have changed the names of most of them, except for the few whose roles were of sufficiently high profile to make it impossible for their real identities to be missed. I welcome all those who recognize themselves in this story to get onto the Internet and say whether I have been fair to them. I hope I have been.

I stepped into the nomination process in October 2009. Between that time and a Christmas party at the end of the year, I encountered a few hiccups, but by the end of December my optimism was soaring. I describe what happened in those three months at the website www.runningforparliament.com. My diary, also accessible at that site, is a day-to-day account of increasingly desperate efforts to get ready for an election that might have come at any time.

The Conservative government of the day was in a minority position in the House of Commons. Every day I was not ready meant, for me, another day I risked public embarrassment. The main opposition party, the Liberal Party of Canada, had served notice that it would move to defeat the Conservatives in any way that it could. As it happened, the election was called only in late March of 2011, and voting day would be five weeks later. By then I had been the Conservative Party of Canada's designated candidate for the riding of Ottawa–Vanier for nineteen months. The intensity had never let up.

My decision to get into this in the first place may have been a folly. I did not really need to see what I saw. I need not have learned what I learned. My career was going well, my income was high, and business at my firm was booming. But I am proud of what I took on and proud of having gone the distance.

To now keep quiet is, for me, not an option. Near the end of this book, I offer a number of observations and conclusions which I believe are important. The book also works toward a simple quiz for novices. If I had rated myself on the quiz before running, I would have thought twice about it.

I had always been interested in participatory politics, though I had rarely been active in political party associations. I was more active in Liberal Party politics when my working life began than I was in Conservative circles, but my time in Liberal Party ranks was decades ago. By 2009, I had been a regular contributor to the financial coffers of the Conservative Party for thirty years. When I filled in my Nomination Contestant Questionnaire and submitted it to the National Candidate Election Committee for the Conservative Party of Canada (CPC), it seemed to hit the key competencies the CPC was looking for.

I am a graduate of Canada's Royal Military College and served eight years in the military; I had been a doctoral student, teaching assistant, and sessional lecturer on political theory at Carleton University in Ottawa for four years; when active in the Liberal Party of Canada, I was executive assistant to a minister in the government of Pierre Trudeau; I had been part of two commissions focused on the future of our country (the Drury Inquiry, on the future of the Northwest Territories, and the Task Force on Canadian Unity); I had been a public servant for twenty-two years and reached the rank of acting assistant deputy minister while with Canada's Department of National Defence; and, for the past seven years, I had been associate vice-president with CRG Consulting, a mid-sized consulting firm with a nationwide clientele.

On the community service front, I am the founding president of the Real Property Institute of Canada; I was on the executive of the Sharbot Lake Property Owners' Association (my wife, Marie, and I now own the cottage my parents built); and I was active in local sports when my two boys were involved in soccer and hockey. The national office of the CPC believed my being bilingual (I grew up in Quebec City) and an immigrant (from the Netherlands) would also be pluses in my run for Parliament.

Ever since my time in a Liberal minister's office, I had had, at the back of my mind, the notion that I would be a worthy candidate for Parliament. The minister I worked with had encouraged me to consider this. But all I ever did in the subsequent thirty years was attend the odd party meeting (always the Conservative Party). I came away from those meetings every time with a sense that — while I believed I could be good as a politician — I was not the kind of person who builds the networks required to get there. Without a network, as a general rule, entry into politics on the side of one of Canada's national political parties is almost impossible.

In the summer of 2009 I was reading a biography written by Ian Kershaw, titled *Hitler*. It is a 1,500-page book. I undertook the reading of it as a project because, ever since military college, one of my areas of great fascination was the turn within Germany, after the Great War, to the politics of fear and terror introduced by Adolf Hitler and the Nazis. My parents and their families in the Netherlands had seen the disintegration of democratic principles and ideals first-hand. The impact on them, and therefore on me, was to entrench an undercurrent of unease about civil society. Things can go belly up very quickly.

I have always wondered how a reasonably well-educated population could have fallen into the frenzy of German politics in the 1930s. I frequently asked myself, "What kind of person would I have been had I been born into that time and place?" Kershaw describes in great detail the forces that can take individuals and societies in a direction where democracy of the many cedes its place to the absolute authority of the few. I asked myself whether it would be possible in a country such as Canada for individuals and communities to abandon their right to have meaningful influence over the political decisions that affect their daily lives.

I was just coming to the end of Kershaw's book when I read a notice from the CPC electoral district association in my riding that it was forming a 400 Club to support the promotion of conservative values and principles in Ottawa–Vanier. What better way to ensure that democratic values are maintained than to participate in what I thought, naively, would be a readers' club of like-minded individuals? I would learn soon enough that the 400 in 400 Club referred not to a target number of interested people but to a fundraising dollar amount, pure and simple.

I knew very little about the Ottawa–Vanier Conservative Association, though I had always paid a membership fee and contributed annually to the federal party since the late 1980s. While never gravitating to the right wing of the party (I held back my contributions in the years when conservatism in Canada was dominated by the Reform Party), I have always found comfort in the broad principles of conservatism.

From time to time these same principles had led me to view favourably (working with and voting for) the Liberal Party of Canada. The Liberals often espoused conservative principles when governing. But I always knew that my attraction to the Liberal Party was impermanent. I was a conservative, through and through. And if a time comes when a person has the opportunity to personally and publicly stand for a political party, I believe that one's own political orientation must line up as well as possible with the philosophical underpinnings of the political party one stands for.

My political vision begins with the situation in our riding of Ottawa–Vanier in the nation's capital. While political "vision" is typically cast at the regional and national levels, Ottawa–Vanier is a kind of microcosm of Canada itself. We have a fairly large immigrant community (about 12%), our francophone population is about 30%, the Aboriginal population is equal to the 3% it is nationally, and we actually have the largest population of Inuit south of the treeline. Our incomes range from the highs in Rockcliffe and Rothwell Heights to the lows in Vanier. Thanks to the work of concerned citizens and community associations, our crime rate is about average (though concentrated in a few areas), and so on.

My vision of Canada, based upon solutions for the riding of Ottawa–Vanier, is of a country where meaningful dialogue is enthusiastically fostered within communities and across the riding. The tools for this would be traditional media and the welter of contemporary Internet options. The encouragement for this dialogue would come from elected officials who would use their public platforms to ask ten times as many questions as they undertake to answer. As an elected official, leading by example, I would have expected to attend public events in one part of the riding and encourage residents in the other parts to stop by for a visit. I would have become a regular at our farmers' markets, cultural displays, theatre evenings, restaurants, businesses, leisure events, university and college public lectures, and so on.

Ottawa–Vanier is a single electoral district but really a collection of separate and disparate parts linked together for the sole purpose of numbers and polls. Nonetheless, I think federal politicians should begin with the reality of their riding, whatever the bureaucratic reasons for its creation, and work to build a community out of it. Physical contact between people is a pretty good way to begin and maintain a process which has people care about their neighbours and about the well-being of their community as a whole. There is a range of benefits associated with this, not least of these being economic benefits.

While community-building may not be a direct way to improve the distribution of economic surplus, I think increased use of local goods and services by people who are neighbours will help. For example, Rockcliffe and Rothwell Heights residents shopping in the Beechwood or Vanier farmers' markets can make a difference.

While thoughts like this may seem naive, if we stop thinking along these lines, we are at ever greater risk of losing our collective confidence. For Canada as a whole, the collective confidence and camaraderie that become palpable during events like the winter 2010 Olympics would be only a chimera if federal politicians did not dare to be naive about what it takes to achieve mutual regard on an ongoing basis.

I think that the increasing globalization of economies and cultures will lead to a breakdown of our societies unless we nurture locally the energy and the motivation to keep holding hands (physically) and talking (orally) within political units that remain small enough to be "real." I think Canada is small enough to be real. I think Ottawa–Vanier is certainly small enough. Just as the individual is more effective when strong and confident, just as strong and confident individuals are more likely to emerge from loving and supportive structures than from atomized relationships, I believe that groups of people are more effective globally if they work well and effectively together locally.

I guess you'd call me a small-c conservative. A conservative, to my mind, is one who values precedent. We also deplore poverty, deplore inequality of opportunity, deplore waste of private and public goods. Conservatives are like most other thinking and feeling Canadians on these scores and others.

A conservative has an inherent faith that most people, given a choice, will do what is best for themselves, their families, and their communities. Provide me with a reasonably level playing field, and I will try awfully hard. We conservatives, when in government, want to set the stage (via laws, regulations, policies, government actions, and so on) so that people can compete in the marketplace of ideas, goods, and services with a reasonable equality in opportunity. We believe the result will be more positive if any one of us, or groups of us, are then able to figure things out for ourselves rather than have the answers imposed upon us by someone else.

When we look about and see that the system does not work for everyone, we conservatives expect governments to take action to catch and support those who are failing. Doing so, however, risks having the recipients of that support move into dependency relationships with government, and that will seal their fates.

Conservatives are generally thought of as self-interested, and indeed we are! But my self-interest is worth nothing if I or members of my family become victims of a crime which arises from societal unfairness that could have been fixed. It is interesting that Conservative governments in Canada introduced community-minded measures such as the minimum wage, social welfare, unemployment insurance, credit agencies, control over the banking industry (under Prime Minister Bennett), women's right to vote (Borden), Aboriginal people's right to vote, the first Bill of Rights (Diefenbaker), a realistic environmental regime (Mulroney), free trade, and so on.

In a discussion I had at an event with some new Canadians from Poland, the immigrant attendees added that a conservative is remarkable because he or she is prepared to say that something is right and something is wrong. I have never had a problem staking out my position on the issues in front of me. Conservatives are often viewed as people who insist upon "black and white" approaches to life's problems, but that is not the whole story: there is a great deal of difference between conservatism and dogmatism. I view a declaratory statement about something being right or wrong as clarity that is needed at the start of a debate. For a dogmatist, it is also the end of the debate.

I told myself that throughout my time as a candidate for political office, I would have many opportunities to say what my perspectives meant in terms of government policies, regulations, laws, and overall conduct. When confronted with specific questions, I would always ask, "What would a conservative do?" This gave me a solid starting position, though it was not at all certain that I would stay with that position when different perspectives raised in the course of discussion impressed themselves upon me.

I should say that none of my political opinions has particular relevance for the observations and recommendations in the concluding chapters of this book. I share them with you because one cannot be a candidate for public office without having political views. I want to be transparent about mine. What matters later in this book is what I will have to say about the mechanics of running in an election. Those mechanics are essentially the same for everyone.

My diary recounts one person's six hundred days of engagement in the nitty-gritty world of volunteers, political staffers, and sitting politicians. Folk such as these and their cohorts across the land together constitute the lifeblood of democracy in Canada. In every federal and provincial election, hundreds of people step into the political world for the first time. Every one of them has a story to tell.

Unfortunately, candidates' stories about the electoral process in Canada — when told at all — are told by those who win. This is unfortunate because the winners' perspectives are coloured by a human need to ascribe real meaning to results which often have almost nothing to do with individual candidates' efforts. The perspective of the candidates who lost, who outnumber the winners by a factor of five and more, are silenced by a lack of interest in what they have to say. To the victors go the spoils, along with all the intellectual attention we humans can muster.

Potential candidates who are the primary target of the advice in this book are much more likely to lose than to win. The unsuccessful novice is silenced not only by the collective disinterest which immediately follows the reporting of election results but also by the imperative to get back to work. There is a whole lot of money for him or her to recover, not to mention the esteem of professional colleagues and the personal time with family and friends that had to be set aside.

If it were physically possible to gather the stories of everyone who has been active in the political process, it would be instructive to draw out common themes. Those common themes could then be linked to the theories espoused by experts who spend their lives wrestling with the issues involved. The ideal would be to achieve a resonance in the thinking and emotions of millions of citizens who — whether they know it or not — have reason to care about what is happening in the political space all around them.

This book is also written, therefore, for the countless individuals who wonder from time to time what happens when their governments undergo the scrutiny and renewal that elections are meant to provide. Does it really matter who the candidates are in any particular electoral district? When, during an election, you meet at the door a person who says "Hello to you, please vote for me," what were the machinations which propelled that person from his or her private life onto your doorstep? If that person is standing for one of the established political parties whose policies and programs are being bombarded at you every hour of every day, why does he or she appear to believe that thirty seconds of your time together is important rather than simply irritating?

I have my own answers. But remember: they emerge from a single set of experiences. Readers are invited to infuse their own practical experiences and to find their separate ways to contribute to a political dialogue that, in my view, has to get kick-started. The success of this book will lie in the extent to which readers who have themselves been candidates for public office say "That happened to me too!" or fire up their laptops and tell me I am wrong. Its success will grow when observers of Canadian democracy see reasons to revisit what they have already learned from other sources. Citizens who want to know what motivates that stranger who knocks on their door during an election will, if the book is successful, better appreciate the candidate's efforts. Thirty seconds at your door is enough time for you to offer them a smile and a word or two of encouragement.

On the day of the vote, May 2, 2011, I lost the election. I obtained just over 27% of the vote in my riding. That I lost was not a surprise. Ottawa–Vanier has been a Liberal stronghold since the riding was created in 1923. It is said by many political observers to be the safest Liberal seat in the country. Why read a book written by a candidate who lost?

My answer is that if Canadians want to have the option of voting for people who have spent their working lives somewhere other than politics, the electoral process needs to be improved. As things stand, the process is unfair to novices. Winners, the ones who may be on their way to becoming career politicians, have a stake in maintaining the status quo within the mechanisms that brought to them their victories. Even the widely lauded proposals of the sitting member of Parliament representing Wellington–Halton Hills, Michael Chong, were designed with the re-election of Michael Chong somewhere deep in his mind. Life is that way.

The losers know that the impact of the different tests put to all candidates in the course of an election is far more severe upon novices with career backgrounds outside of politics than upon young politicos and their seniors, the career politicians. If nothing changes, fewer and fewer novices will stand for election in the future.

When commentators in the media, in academia, and on city streets lament that "good people do not go into politics," the people whose absence they lament are surely novices like me. They mean people who have lived a life outside of politics, who have demonstrated competence and integrity, who have made a contribution through their professional and personal efforts that has reflected back upon their own characters. They mean well-rounded individuals.

I believe that a continued drift toward the professionalization of politics is linked to the slides in voter turnout at the polls and in public participation in politics between elections. The disconnect between ordinary citizens and a political class will continue to grow if we see fewer and fewer of our own kind in the ranks of newly elected members of provincial and federal legislatures.

An electoral process that is more fair for novices is likely to draw more good people into the fray. And changes that impose greater fairness are more likely to be inspired by those of us who have lost. The losers want to level the playing field. The losers want to remove structural obstacles that appeared easier for the victors to overcome. We conservatives, I could add, are motivated to make these kinds of improvements. Only when the opportunity to pursue important goals is equal for everyone can we conservatives confidently say that all people are personally responsible for what they do with the opportunities that come their way.

Oops. That sounds like a polemicist talking again, doesn't it? Rest assured, from here on in I will try to not let that happen too often — the Conservative Party of Canada will not like what I have to say in this book any more than the other mainstream political parties. The electoral system in Canada greatly favours career politicians. Unless you are okay with that, you will agree with me that the time has come to do something about it.

A nationally acclaimed political science professor and friend of mine, with whom I shared my experience, observed that my book will not provide much of an inducement for people with solid backgrounds outside of politics to enter into the ring. Yet my purpose is not to discourage others from taking on the challenge. My purpose, if you are poised to become a novice candidate as I was, is to help you get ready by providing a "heads up" on what to expect. For us, politics always meant something other than a lifetime job and a pension. Fair play begins with us novice competitors having a realistic idea about what lies ahead.

CHAPTER 1.

DOWN THE RABBIT HOLE

To prove yourself in any line of work takes at least twenty years of challenges missed and met, risks endured and overcome, failures acknowledged and successes acclaimed.

Most of my working life had been spent outside the context of the unique structures and functions which bear upon elections in a democratic country. I thought that running in a federal election would give me the opportunity to display the qualifications I had picked up over the years. I would use the period before and during the election to explain to my riding's residents why and how a person such as I could make a useful contribution in the House of Commons. The thought that I risked being beaten up never crossed my mind.

I learned that running for election in Canada, certainly at the federal and provincial levels, is akin to running a gauntlet. A series of tests is administered during the electoral process, tests that can be likened to the blows administered by sailors of old upon their hapless victims. Of course, the situation is not quite that desperate. But it sure felt that way a lot of the time to me.

The gauntlet can also be likened to the obstacle course I and my colleagues had to run through at Canada's Royal Military College before we were accepted as full-fledged members of the Cadet Wing. That obstacle course, run by one recruit class after another for well over one hundred years, consists of tests that range from ducking under fallen stumps in frigid waters to crawling through extensive fields of mud plowed through with pig manure and climbing over structures, sprayed with muck and oil, that are high enough to break a recruit's leg should he or she fall. At RMC, the obstacle course is run together by entire squadrons, consisting of thirty or forty recruits at a time, who help each other out. Victory at the end is collective.

Running the gauntlet of an election, however, is a solitary process for the runner. Although the advisors and handlers are like RMC's third- and fourth-year cadets, who shout encouragement from the sidelines as the recruits struggle to prove their mettle and to maintain their dignity, elections are a solitary process because there is only one candidate for each party and because representatives of the other parties in a riding have no interest — none whatsoever — in helping one another. The failure of all others running in the same race is the goal of every person who hopes to win.

The tests in the election gauntlet are not the physical tests set up for RMC recruits to prevail under, through, and over. They are mostly metaphysical. The runner is tested with regard to his or her hold on privacy, personal values, commitment to the race, leadership, endurance, isolation, and — at the end — determination to succeed. On the face of it, there would seem to be no comparison between gauntlets lined with sticks and stones and a gauntlet lined with words. But both can hurt.

I nonetheless believe that testing candidates for public office is essential. If the trappings of democracy continue to wither away, I argue in this book, the tests in the gauntlet should be held sacrosanct. It should not be possible for a person to step into an elected position and hold sway over fellow citizens if that person has not been jostled by his or her peers in the moral and intellectual equivalent of a gauntlet. Winning a majority of votes from all those citizens who go to the polls should remain the last of the rites of passage.

The candidates who are best equipped for their run through

the gauntlet are the men and women I call "politicos." Experienced politicos are often called "career politicians." I describe politicos in greater detail in the next chapter.

First-time politicos run through the gauntlet at a faster clip than novices can. They have more padding against the blows. They emerge — whether successful in their goal to win a seat in Parliament or not — with fewer scrapes. Career politicians have been through it all before. They know what to expect, their funding base is secure, their election material and their name signs — even if tattered on account of previous use — are ready to go.

I want to see more novice candidates run the gauntlet and, when they do, I want them to have a better time in the process than I had. I want to help them see into the future. I offer this book as an eye-opener.

To be a "novice candidate" means not only that you are getting into the electoral process for the first time. It also means you do not have a family background in politics. You are not following the footsteps of a parent or a grandparent who has, around the dinner table or through family lore, let you know what to expect. You are not networked within the structures of the political party you are about to represent on the public stage. You may even have altogether avoided being identified with one political party or another, may have kept your political leanings private until now. All this is about to change.

How much the change will affect you and your views about politics depends to a great degree upon what you thought elections were all about before you ever got this far. Notwithstanding my studies of and readings of politics, and notwithstanding my participation in politically relevant activities during my career, I learned only in running that my own mental image of the electoral process had been delusional. I still believed in a fable.

In this fable, Canada's legislative assemblies are filled with people representing a cross-section of the population. All these people have earned their place by convincing those who voted for them that, on balance, they will be pretty darned good representatives of the common interest. Not every voter's interests can be represented, of course. The elected representatives you see in those imagined assemblies are mature enough and astute enough to speak for a greater commonality in views than the competing candidates had been able to do. Furthermore, every successful candidate belongs to a political party which has gathered together a large number of like-minded Canadian citizens. The platform and policies of these political parties can be counted upon to reflect a consensus among tens of thousands of citizens who voted for one of the representatives that now sit with their respective parties in the legislature.

To run in an election in this fabled world, a potential candidate must know his or her riding extremely well. Occasionally, young adults will step into the ring with very little practical experience in the wider world of social challenges and commerce. But those few will be exceptional individuals who have a preternatural ability to connect with others and to speak publicly for the hopes and dreams of fellow citizens. More candidates will be men or women approaching, or well into, middle age. All of them, though, will be amazingly energetic.

The role of an elected representative was recently described by a sitting member of Parliament as not a job, but a set of functions. Elected representatives need energy and good health to carry out those functions. In Ottawa–Vanier, the functions begin with regular, extensive, and ongoing engagement with up to sixty thousand residents and myriad organizations, public gatherings, and events.

To be effective in an election requires a large support network. In my imagined world, that network consists of experienced, dedicated people who know the intricacies of the electoral process. They are active members of established political parties' local organizations, and they know what to do when candidates, first-time or repeat, arrive on their doorstep. They have the expertise and money ready to ensure that their candidate becomes widely known among riding residents. It is their pleasure to usher their new candidate to residents' doors and to the podium in front of neighbourhood organizations to talk about party politics and riding issues.

Talking about politics happens between candidates and members of the voting public, in this world, every time they meet. These discussions are respectful because the public recognizes in the candidate both a person who is much like they are and someone whose background is sure to earn attention and respect. Everyone in this imagined world knows that politics matter. Everyone is proud of the candidate because of what he or she has taken on.

Within the political party that the candidate will stand for is a shared understanding on the political issues of the day. The party's platform and, for the party which forms the government of the day, the government's policies are tabled for aspiring and selected candidates. The contents of those platforms and policies are always open for discussion. Proposals from candidates are always taken seriously. People in central party positions, you see, know that platforms and policies play out differently in local riding settings. Remember, this is a fable.

The ways in which those positions are communicated are always open for revision. The purpose of a party, and the purpose of a government, is to speak coherently through its representatives to ordinary citizens all across the land. By carefully framing its explanations, and by each party's representatives being mature and open-minded individuals, even the hundreds of thousands of voters who do not support the winning candidate in an election will feel that the continuing process of governance is legitimate. People are being listened to. People know they can have influence.

In the race for public office, in the running of the gauntlet of tests, the competition is guided by regulations and law to be as equal as possible for every candidate in the race. Even so, there are limitations.

There will always be an advantage, for example, for the candidate who won in the previous election and who has been sitting in the legislature as the riding's representative. That person will usually have had four or more years to make personal contact with riding residents from a position of influence and profile that other candidates standing for election cannot hope to have achieved. But this can work both ways. Depending upon the sitting representative's performance, incumbency may not be an advantage: it may actually have a negative effect. Furthermore, if the sitting representative is a member of the governing party, the successes and failures of the government itself will have to be explained to local audiences.

To counter the natural advantage of the sitting representative, I expected to see no regulatory or legal obstacles preventing potential candidates from moving about the riding between elections to meet with residents and to share rivalling political perspectives.

Rival candidates preparing for the next election cannot hope to match the publicly funded newsletters sent out by sitting representatives to every home in the riding. They cannot rise up to the public profile elected members earn from years of public events. Since I knew there was public money supporting a sitting politician's riding office, however, I thought there would be money for potential rivals to have an office as well.

The truth, unfortunately, is that fairness in the electoral process is a myth. Worse still, it appears we are headed down a track toward the irrelevancy of candidates as conveyors of public will and interest. It is time to put the fable aside and look at what really happens.

If nothing changes, it will ultimately no longer matter who the candidates are at all. Winning or losing will be a result either of lottery or of a locked-in outcome determined by the advantages of incumbency. It will be possible for candidates in a province like Quebec to be elected at the federal level if they have no prior association with their riding whatsoever, or if they cannot speak French. (Wait a minute! That's already happened, hasn't it?) It is already true that a third of elected incumbents at the federal level can expect to stay in office long enough to build up large pensions. If a person represents a party in a riding that has always voted along that party's lines, that person is sure to win again and again regardless of individual merit.

In a December 2014 article in the *New York Times Magazine*, the columnist Binyamin Appelbaum observed that wealthy individuals and firms who want to influence political decision-making in the United States now spend ten times more to influence the policy-making process than they do, by financing a preferred candidate, to influence who wins or loses. They do this because, to privileged people who care about the content of laws and policies, who the candidate is no longer matters. I will be getting back to those privileged people in a moment.

In this darkening reality of democracy, the directions set by government leaders are less and less responsive to what candidates stand for and for whom they speak. The electorate already know this. Voter turnout is low and, unless legislated as a legal imperative, will continue to reduce. The public's interest in meeting potential candidates and talking politics with them will fade away to nil, whether voting is an imperative or not. The interest on the part of members of political party associations in talking politics with their own potential or selected candidates will move to zero as well. Novice candidates who have the professional background and courage to talk back to party leaders will not be welcome in party ranks.

In such a situation — one that approaches hopelessness — almost all members of the public and most candidates have their eyes focused upon what is happening centrally. The age-old debate about delegation or representation at the riding level no longer has much meaning. Policy adjustment and change through ongoing public engagement become quaint ideas. The only thing that really matters is what central party headquarters wants to do. Headquarters counts upon candidates to get it done.

The democracy that I dreamed about does not exist. The

address of my electoral district association office at #5 Beechwood Avenue was a small box behind the Canada Post counter in the New Edinburgh Pharmacy.

In our much darker world, a voter votes only for the party. Very little intellectual effort is made by residents at their doors to distinguish candidates from the parties they represent. A person with a respectable professional background such as I had, with the extent of community involvement that I could claim on professional grounds alone, can be told at the door of a well-heeled and educated Rothwell Heights resident to "get off my property before I shoot you!"

In a dark world such as this, it is no longer an honour to run for public office.

In this world, Canadians know that candidates matter in the legislature only if they are selected by the leaders of mainstream political parties to join governing cliques or cabinets. Canadian citizens with solid backgrounds, the "good people" whom pundits and columnists want to see enter into public life, have become unwelcome, notwithstanding what they can bring into legislative assemblies. The "good people" will become less interested anyway in pursuing positions for which the odds are either random or stacked. Their welcome is all the less because independence of mind in a candidate makes it more difficult for political parties to impose a franchise-type control over electoral district associations. Their willingness is all the less because Canadians already see, from watching how elected officials in their legislatures behave, what powerlessness and dishonour look like.

But so what? If our country continues to hum along, the economy remains reasonably strong, people's rights are reasonably well preserved, a majority of citizens still manage to hold down reasonable jobs for reasonable pay, so what?

To my mind, the problem is vulnerability.

A successful democracy is a regime of structures and functions — political, social, and economic — that reflects the intelligence and the character of the many citizens who make it up. It is not a regime which gives a free hand to decide how domestic and international pressures upon society will be dealt with to only a few. Fair elections are one of the levers available to the many. Elections send representatives of the many into public office; the few who take up powerful positions are selected from these. If elections cease to be fair, if "good people" lose interest in standing for elections, and if the many stop voting, the few will become a cohort of like-minded individuals who increasingly lose touch with the intelligence and character of large swaths of citizens.

A drift toward government by the few over the many puts democracy itself at risk. Our vulnerability is greater still, unfortunately, because a similar drift toward concentration of power is happening down a parallel track.

Apologists for income inequality correctly affirm that the gap between the rich and the poor in Canada is not extreme relative to the rest of the world and to many other democracies. The data also show that, in the early years of this century, the gap is closing rather than growing. Nonetheless, there is an accumulation of wealth at the very top, and the size of that accumulation is getting more extreme.

The French economist Thomas Piketty, author of *Capital in the Twenty-First Century* (2014), has demonstrated that a slow but inexorable increase is underway in the concentration of capital all across the planet. In most countries, capital is concentrated in the hands of fewer than 1% of citizens. Wealth is being accumulated within the families of those few citizens, an accumulation that will progressively outstrip what world economies provide to everyone else through economic growth. This is because, historically and contemporaneously, the growth of value for capital assets is 4% or higher annually but the growth of economies is half that or less.

What the 1% will do with their money a few decades from now can already be known by looking at what they are doing today. More and more private money — wealth that is protected and grows behind barriers of domestic tax laws and international banking codes of silence — will be used by the billionaire families to achieve social and political results that serve their own economic purposes. This means that if schools and universities turn out too many sociologists or lawyers who challenge the impact of poverty on the vast majority of global residents, those institutions will be compromised, challenged, or replaced by entrepreneurial alternatives. In all of North America, the charter school movement will grow. In all developed societies, private money will displace public money to a greater and greater extent. If you or I belonged to the 1%, we would behave in the same way. The will of the few, of the billionaires and their families, will bowl over the will of the many — unless the many are strong in their own right. That, again, is how life is.

The strength of the many lies in the effectiveness of elected governments. Pushback to the billionaires can come from elected representatives, working together under attentive prime ministers and presidents who themselves have been tested by the people in fair and equal elections.

The risk in our current system, however, is that political power may become co-opted by those few who hold the preponderance of financial power. The crossover between politics and wealth must be avoided.

Sarah Chayes (*Thieves of State*, 2015) observes that politics in failed and failing democracies have long been a route to wealth. Without a values-based core of elected politicians in their legislatures, she warns, governments can become little more than fronts for "vertically organized criminal organizations." If the worst has happened, if a government has become rather like "a crime syndicate in disguise," good people will stay as far away as they can.

One way to become a plutocrat in Russia is to become a senior elected official. It is not impossible to imagine a future in Canada when the desire of elected representatives to be part of the 1% overwhelms a prime minister to the point where he or she will accept large envelopes filled with cash in order to kick-start a private life after politics. It is not impossible to imagine former government ministers and former premiers becoming pals with one-percenters who have themselves used political office to win new friends and influence people — with money rather than with argument. I bet that one day we might even see plutocrats who run giant communications firms gain their way into elected office and get positioned so that they can assume the highest public office in their governments. Sitting prime ministers may one day brazenly direct public funds to golf courses owned by millionaire friends or launch public ad campaigns which enrich still more the wealthy few among a leader's friends. You never know. It could happen.

We are not yet fully into the dark world of democracy in Canada, but we are headed in that direction. Strong candidates who know a world outside of politics, if given a reasonable chance to win public office in fair elections, can help to stop the drift.

To allow the drift toward greater and greater inequality in the electoral process go unaddressed, to not talk back to power centres that are too easily seduced into strategies that help those at the centre become part of the 1%, requires experienced and courageous people to gather around. To stand up in a legislature is one of the best ways to have the needed effect. And in order to stand up in a legislature, it is first necessary to run the gauntlet.

If nothing is done, you see, the future will, one day, require a major course correction. This will be an awful thing to behold. Piketty observes that such course corrections have, historically, always been catastrophic events such as the French Revolution or the twentieth century's world wars. At some point, the many have had enough. At some point, they rediscover their collective strength. Out of shared desperation and disgust, they storm the offices of the plutocrats and political leaders and they raid the homes of their families.

There are alternative course-correction strategies suggested in books written by thinkers and philosophers today that can, however, be digested and managed only by people who have lived a real life, who are mature enough to provide leadership as well as management skills. If people like you and I dodge the opportunity to run for public office, we will be ceding our place to the politicos without a fight. Not only are those people mostly young and inexperienced, but a remarkable number do not read books. The Internet and the superficial communication of Twitter have not done the complexity of our societies any favours. Politicos are not bad people, but without a substantial presence of experienced outsiders in the ranks of our political institutions, our governments will not be able to maintain a perspective that balances party ideologies, political opportunism, and reality.

That is why I sincerely hope that my friend the political science professor was wrong when he assessed that my story will discourage others from running. "Others like you," he said to me, "will not want to descend into that unique context within which elections are won and lost."

In my case, I slipped down the rabbit hole almost by accident and made do as well as I could. I learned that in the arcane world of participatory politics, the unique mix of structures and functions of Canada's electoral process have become dangerously beguiling to those comfortable within its shadowy bounds. In discussion with others I have likened this to Plato's cave analogy in his classic work *Republic*; those who are fully subscribed to the electoral system are like the cave dwellers. I stayed half in and half out of that cave for quite a while, often to my wife's chagrin, and challenged myself to speak on the inside about what I had experienced in the world outside. Because I was unprepared to deal entirely on the cave dwellers' terms with their logic and schemes, I was not well suited to the gauntlet..

We need novice candidates who have a sober yet eager sense of what is needed to carry Canada's democratic institutions into the middle and second half of this century and beyond. We need novice candidates who are more prepared than I was to succeed.

My story is meant to help you peer through the veil into what will happen when you sign up to run. If you can see what is about to happen, if you have braced yourself, you are certain to do better than I did.

The image of the gauntlet that I use throughout this story draws from origins where killing the participant was very much the intent. The victim was usually a person who had been found guilty of one crime or another. The gauntlet engaged the victim's peers in a collective punishment that compromised the punishers: their slaying of a peer reinforced the message "This will happen to you if you don't behave!"

You the novice, however, have not done anything wrong. Nor had I. I must nevertheless plead guilty to not being ready for the tests that came my way. That is why they hurt more than they need to have done. If you are prepared, if you are ready, your run for public office may actually strengthen your resolve to stay in the game and to try again if you lose.

The ordering of tests in the chapters that follow — privacy, values, commitment, leadership, endurance, isolation, accomplishment — reflects the order of intensity with which the tests revealed themselves to me as I ran. In actual fact, in the course of my five-hundred-page diary the tests are intermingled and overlap each other. Any given structure, event, or set of circumstances can engage more than one specific test. During the last of the tests, all of the other six are run concurrently. Bear with me, therefore, when a situation described once or twice before is returned to for a second or third time. The test I elaborate upon each time will be different.

No matter how well you, the novice, prepare yourself, the odds against you winning will unfortunately remain long, for all the reasons that I describe in this book. But let's get going. The hell with the odds, and damn the torpedoes!

CHAPTER 2.

THE TEST OF PRIVACY

So, a serious opportunity has come your way to become a candidate for public office and you have decided to take it up. It was not a bluff. It was not a taunt. You know intuitively that you are at the very beginning of something, but you cannot possibly know what that "something" will entail. You have always had an interest in politics, and you have always valued the place of political structures in the stability and vibrancy of nations. But you have not been working your way toward this opportunity. You are naive about the political process. You are a novice.

One of the first things you must realize is that the novice is a rare bird in this business.

In their book *Tragedy in the Commons: Former Members of Parliament Speak Out about Canada's Failing Democracy*, Alison Loat and Michael MacMillan observe that most elected representatives, in their personal narratives, say their entry into politics was unplanned. But the truth is that most candidates running for public office for the first time can fairly be called "politicos." They are people who began to devote their lives to social and political activism at an early age. It is not unusual to see featured in the curriculum vitae of a sitting politician, at the municipal, provincial, or federal level, that he or she became active in some notable way while still a student at university, if not in high school. Though the average age of elected politicians is fifty-two, some have had no life — some not even a job — outside of politics at all, and their number is growing.

For someone like you, the priority coming out of high school or university was to secure in the workaday world a place upon which you could begin to build a reputation and a career. You did not want your reputation to be associated with a political party "brand"; you did not want your developing career or business to be placed at risk every four years when elections come around. While you may have taken an interest in politics during your youth, perhaps even an intense interest, for most of your career until now you were apolitical in how you conducted your day-to-day affairs. Your social and political activism was mostly behind the scenes. You most likely limited your political engagement to financial contributions to the political party of your choice. Your decision to stand for election will be a surprise to all who know you.

The fact that you are seriously contemplating an unexpected opportunity to run in an upcoming election confirms that you have long harboured in the back of your mind the possibility that this might happen.

There are a great many characteristics associated with other first-time candidates for public office, however, that you do not share. Remember: most of those others got the bug early, and committed themselves to a strong interplay of social and political activism when they were teenagers. When *they* step up to the plate for the first time, either by choice or as a concession to others, it is not a surprise to anyone.

The winner in a federal or provincial election will sit among the legislators who vote our legal and regulatory regimes into place. It is an awesome responsibility. Yet it is not at all unusual for first-time candidates to be under thirty years old. Because you have already built an independent career in business, the private sector, or the public sector (perhaps even in all three), you are already in your middle years. When you compare notes with those others, you will learn that while their professional background is unimpressive — if it exists at all — their experience with electoral politics is much more extensive than yours.

The younger and the older politicos alike usually began their political careers in the offices of elected politicians. From there they moved into political party hierarchies at the federal or provincial level. For a few years they then moved back and forth from job to job "on the Hill" at the federal level, or took up support positions in provincial legislative assemblies, and then went back again to the political party they called "home."

Those others, those first-time candidates who are not at all like you, certainly want to win in the next election, but for them winning does not matter very much at an individual level. What really matters is for their party to win. If their party wins, their network of friends and associates will be able to help them secure post-election jobs. Simply to have run for their party, even if they were unsuccessful, was to earn a badge of honour. It will have confirmed a deep commitment to their party's fortunes. It will have earned a reasonable reward.

Your own reputation, on the other hand, will not be built upon by what you are about to do. You have already earned a good reputation, in the line of work upon which you set out so long ago. Your great hope is that among those who watched you earn your spurs, your reputation will not be undone. There is a good chance you will be returning to that fold after this run for public office is over. Indeed, unless your unexpected opportunity to step into active politics is in a riding that is called a "safe seat," meaning that your success in the upcoming election is virtually assured, you, the novice candidate, are most likely to lose. The truth — brace yourself — is that you are almost certain to be about to return to the world from which you have come. If you are, as I am, the type of person who sets aside doubts in order to stay focused you are likely to forget this. I know I did.

Safe seats, by the way, are rarely offered to novices like you and me. Safe seats, when they are vacated by incumbents, become hotly contested by politicos because they know almost for certain that they will be headed to Parliament Hill or to a provincial legislature after the next election has come and gone. A political party will run a novice in a safe seat only if the person is a "star candidate" whose public affiliation will improve the party's own brand. Even then, the novice usually loses. Examples of this are legion.

After you have stepped forward, your privacy will be blown away. In the years after you have run and after you have lost in the next election, it will be impossible to keep much of a distance between what your party stands for and what you may personally believe. If the riding you are running in has been of one political "colour" long enough for that colour to have become an indelible part of local culture, your having stood for one of the other political parties will mark you as an outsider. It will affect you for as long as you stay in the neighbourhood. It will affect every member of your family. It will risk alienating friends. If you are a consultant for a firm which contracts with governments, after you lose the next election, potential clients will wonder if your impartiality can ever again be trusted. Among your friends and family, especially if the party you represented was not popular among them, the hope will be that you regain your senses and crawl back to their side of the political divide.

To this point in your business or public-sector career, it has been important for you to be apolitical in the public sphere. To stand for public office is to cross a line, whether you win or lose.

Your friends and neighbours will ask, "Why the heck are you doing it?" Your family will plead, "Please don't do this to us." Your supervisors in your place of work will say, "Take a leave of absence and good luck." For the novice candidate who hears the call and steps into electoral politics in Canada, a sense of foreboding begins to build, right from the start. At first you will feel euphoria because you have honoured a promise to yourself that was first made decades ago. The euphoria will quickly pass. And then you will fear that perhaps you have really screwed things up, not only for yourself but also for others close to you.

If you are determined to seize this chance to run for public office anyway, you should begin by shoring up your relationships with family, friends, and business associates. Acknowledge to your family that for the duration of your candidacy, a whole lot of what you will be doing will be all about you. Your time to attend to the needs and hurts of others in your private life will be compromised not only by the press of political business but also by the buffeting your ego is about to endure. With friends and colleagues who matter to you, and before your public commitment becomes widely known, reach out to explain what you are about to do and why. Within your firm and with business associates, just be honest: you dare to make this move because you believe your need to take an apolitical stance in all things professional can come to an end.

The politicos, by the way, will have none of those worries. The first-timers and the career politicians alike will have around them families, friends, and colleagues who expect them to seize the chance to run or to run again. They have been close to or part of the world of elected politicians for a very long time. They have taken their measure of what success in politics as a profession means. At the innumerable social and fundraising events they have attended since childhood, their resolve to stay in pursuit of their goal — elected office — was strengthened every time notes were compared or lubricated confessions slurred.

Whereas it will take you time to find your feet in this high-energy world and you will increasingly worry about the impact upon family and friends, the politicos will be pumped and raring to go. You will find their enthusiasm destabilizing because, for you, something far too serious is about to happen to warrant unbridled glee.

I don't mean to be disparaging of politicos. The functions of political leadership can be learned quite quickly by competent men and women. In Canada we have extremely capable public servants who can carry elected officials and ministers until they have gotten the hang of their new roles. Political commentators call for "good people" to step forward, however, because backgrounds of those people give them well-rounded perspectives against which to test what public servants advise.

The opportunity to run for Canada's federal parliament representing the party in power would appear to be an especially meaningful one. In 2009, when the call came to me from the president of the Ottawa–Vanier Electoral District Association, the Conservative Party was the governing party in Ottawa but was in a minority position in the House of Commons. Its leader, Stephen Harper, was the prime minister. The country was at the front end of the winter Olympics that would be held early in 2010 and that would prove to be extremely successful for Canadian athletes. The athletes' success would reflect positively upon the government in Ottawa, upon the party in power, and upon the prime minister of the day.

During my first full year as a designated candidate, however, the government faced challenges which threatened its defeat in Parliament, often on a weekly basis. The Conservatives were lambasted over the treatment of detainees in the ongoing war in Afghanistan; a budget loomed that the opposition in the House said they would defeat no matter what its contents; a prorogation of the House was widely viewed as undemocratic; the leaders of the three other parties in the House threatened a triumvirate that would displace the governing party; and so on. I could no longer keep my opinions about any of this to myself.

The economies of most countries in the developed world had recently collapsed, owing to a loss of confidence in banking institutions right across the globe. But not in Canada. In Canada our banks were strong. Federal regulations over the banking industry had not permitted the highly speculative financing in which banks in other countries had engaged, especially in the United States, Ireland, and Iceland. Canada had been in a balanced federal budget situation and was able to reach out for sovereign loans to finance billions of dollars' worth of infrastructure and other public projects to keep core business activity going strong. Canada was regularly lauded by international think tanks for the competence of its political and institutional management during this time of crisis. The country stood at the top of the OECD in terms of its performance.

To represent a governing political party with that kind of record, one would think, should have been a feather in my cap and made things easier. Going public with my political affiliation should have been a mark of distinction.

But in Ottawa–Vanier, the Conservative Party of Canada was not popular. The party had become known across the country, for example, for a "tough on crime" agenda. In my riding, petty crime such as break-and-enters was an endemic problem. To get tough on crime, rather than be sensitive to the need to turn families and whole communities toward a better state of health, was seen as mean and short-sighted.

The party was known to be suspicious of public servants who had jobs for life and who were perceived to be Liberals in their political orientation, waiting impatiently for the Liberal Party to regain its rightful place as the Governing Party of Canada. Ottawa is a public service town. Canada's public service was the largest employer in my riding.

Meanwhile, among "traditional" Conservatives in my riding, the CPC was thought to have abandoned its small-government principles by engaging in the huge outlay of public dollars that the Action Canada panoply of programs entailed. Action Canada was the banner under which billions of public dollars were spent to construct new roads and buildings, refurbish old ones, and launch infrastructure projects to promote recreation and tourism. That Canada's business community had been saved because of Action Canada was seen by many CPC supporters to be a poor excuse. And perhaps above all, the CPC was still seen to be a western-based organization that would always champion resource exploitation — especially of oil and gas — no matter what the cost to water and air quality, birds landing on tailing ponds, and landscapes.

To represent the governing party in my case was, in the eyes of many voters in Ottawa–Vanier, to stand for the devil. There was a look of "how could you?" in the eyes of many. From a friend of many decades came the words "I would never have guessed that you were one of those!" And my wife, Marie, the eldest daughter in a family of long-standing Liberal persuasion, now had the misfortune of being married to someone like me.

One of my conundrums during the early period after I assumed the role of candidate, even before the significance of my new venture had fully settled in, was how much to say to business associates and clients in my workplace. CRG Consulting did most of its business with the federal government, and here I was about to be outed as a representative of the Conservative Party of Canada.

I didn't resign right away. But, at a meeting in Quebec City in late November 2009, where the issue was the rebuilding (using Action Canada funds) of a historic military armoury that had burned down a few months before, my hesitancy to announce my intentions came to an end. I had to say something. Over a dozen people sat in a large conference room at a hotel a few hundred metres away from the burned-out hulk. Two or three consulting firms were represented, all of us engaged to work together on construction options which could meet a variety of different objectives, including the hosting of concerts on an international scale. The armouries were at the edge of the walls around the old city, backing onto an open park known locally as the Plains of Abraham, and were integrated with another historic structure, the Citadel.

The people in the room included middle-level public servants. Being unaware of my status as a candidate for public office, they let loose for about thirty minutes critiquing their respective ministers and lambasting the Prime Minister's Office, which had taken a particular interest in this project. I knew that I would be meeting with those ministers and the prime minister's staff at a Christmas party scheduled for early December on Parliament Hill. I said nothing about my intentions in the course of the meeting, and I did not engage in the banter and the slander all around me. But I knew that once my intentions became known, the public servants would be worried about my keeping confidences when in political circles, and I knew that in future I should stay away from settings such as this.

When I returned to Ottawa, I advised the president of my firm that I would henceforth remove myself from meetings that included public officials. My firm did a lot of business with governments. It was a simple fact that my being allied publicly with a particular party meant that I and my firm might have drawn fire when future contracts were pursued. If a particularly lucrative contract were to be won, my firm's competitors would charge "unfair competition"; if it were to be lost, my own colleagues might believe "we lost because of your political stripe." I would complete my portion of the work already contracted with Canada and the province of Quebec on the Quebec City armouries, and then I would withdraw from contracts which could put me and my firm in a compromised position.

I would be putting my career on hold — maybe for good — so the opportunity cost in terms of money unearned began to climb. Later you'll read more about the financial toll that my candidacy took on me and my family. Even with an already dawning awareness of what I was getting into, however, saying "no" was no longer an option.

I was introduced to the next round in my life — my life as a candidate for public office — by a number of people I thought I could rely upon to make my transition easier. I learned, however, that I was wrong. Many of my new associates, members of the executive and board of my electoral district association, thought it should be the other way around. Even in the private worlds of their respective professional lives, the few who had full-time jobs believed that my position with CRG Consulting should enable me to direct consulting contracts their way.

Carol Latimer was then the president of my association, Guy DesRoches was charged with fundraising, and Ross Carrothers was the association's treasurer. Like most others playing a substantive role in the association, those three key people were only partially employed or retired. They had the time. They had the interest. And their interest was personal.

Carol had a background in community organization, from when she lived in Calgary. In Ottawa she was involved with contracting firms that sought business from the federal government in the areas of security and public safety. She was a firecracker — short, round, sharp-eyed, fully alive, and energetic. She wanted me to do exactly what she told me to do. She also hoped my position as associate vice-president with CRG Consulting would help her and her professional colleagues to link into new security contracting opportunities. One of my fellow vice-presidents oversaw work we were doing in Afghanistan.

Guy had run for the Progressive Conservatives (as they were in the 1990s) and lost in a northern Ontario riding about ten years earlier. He was a tall, good-looking man, married to an elegant woman, Annette, whose intelligence and determination shone through whenever we spoke. Bilingual, compelling in his personal appearance, and credible because of his background, Guy had a manner of total self-assurance. His approach, however, was often flawed and he had a proclivity to respond to adversity by hurling criticisms at others. His follow-through on undertakings, especially fundraising, was poor. He was not well suited for the role he had agreed to play.

Ross was a former accountant who had held positions in both the private and public sectors. He had been brought into politics, on the side of the Conservative Party, because of a tragedy in his own family, a crime that had gone almost unpunished. He was angry. Ross appeared to know the intricacies of political financing very well. He had been the financial agent for a number of previous CPC candidates in our riding, and I hoped he would play the same role with me. But he and I would have a falling out, largely because — as with Carol — I would insist upon doing things my own way.

Being the candidate meant I had to get comfortable with being known and with talking to anybody and everybody. Even though no election had been called and I was not yet actively campaigning, my days were filled right from the start with the sorts of things that I would continue to do for the next nineteen months, including establishing a public profile online, delivering short speeches, writing letters to the editor, making appearances at public events, lunching with colleagues and potential supporters, knocking on doors, and, of course, fundraising. Remember, in the media, the pundits were either warning of or aggressively calling for an election every other day. I felt the imperative to be ready much more acutely than did the members of my EDA. My personal reputation would be on the line, not theirs.

I therefore began looking about for help. An easy contact for me to make was with Bruce Poulin, candidate of record for the provincial Progressive Conservative Party association in the previous Ontario election and a graduate of RMC about ten years after me. My goal was to obtain from him some names to add to my initial (very short) list of volunteers, but this did not happen. We found ourselves in a restaurant sitting beside an elderly couple who also lived in Rockcliffe and who — the man, at least — were strong Conservative Party supporters. The upshot of the meeting was that Bruce and I reaffirmed our intention to work together. Of the two hours Bruce and I spent together that evening, however, we spent one and a half hours in discussion with our unexpected seatmates. But this, for me, was what I believed politics was all about. It was fun.

I knew it was time to get out of my shell, and get the word out about my candidacy. I needed to access an audience of more than one person or one couple at a time as I had with Bruce Poulin. I wanted to meet with as many neighbourhood organizations in Ottawa–Vanier as I could. After a few false starts, I had given up on EDA volunteers doing research to provide the annotated list I had requested of community associations in our riding. I wanted to see, at a glance, which groups were operating in which neighbourhoods, when they held their meetings, who the contact persons were (including names and numbers of presidents or CEOs, if known), and what issues dominated each group's agenda. The EDA had never had such a document. In the end I pulled the information together myself, spending multiple days surfing the web and reading the *EMC* (a local paper) to create a contact list.

I met with local business leaders, school groups, and arts organizations. I would show up without invitation because EDA volunteers were not available to scout things out and prepare my way. A weeknight visit to the Vanier Beautification committee went very well. I usually limited my role to a self-introduction, after which I would sit and listen to what others had to say. Each of these visits was informative, but I couldn't help but feel while I listened at this one that I was a bit of a fake in this political job. Many of those folks had long taken community living much more seriously than I ever had. They had been working actively to improve their public space, and when different views were expressed, they worked hard to achieve mutual respect among fellow small business and community leaders. For my part, I had dropped into my role as candidate for a federal political party only by happenstance. I was not a community-level leader equal to many of those I spoke with, that's for sure.

One day, one of the EDA board members, Eleanor Brady, mentioned the government's decision to prorogue Parliament in the middle of a growing debate about treatment of Afghan detainees by members of the Canadian Forces. It was a highly unpopular decision in my riding and in much of the rest of the country. I elaborated upon why I was not bothered by it. Eleanor and Carol, who listened in, liked my explanation and asked me to write it down in letter format, addressed to the editor of one of our local papers. It couldn't hurt to get my name out there in print, they said.

I include the letter here not to persuade readers that the government's position on the matter was correct (it was roundly condemned by most political commentators and pundits) but because it reflects the effort I would always make to understand my party's initiatives in terms of my personal orientation to politics. This letter was my first foray into the public sphere on an issue that I would ordinarily have debated privately, with Marie.

LETTER TO THE EDITOR

I was asked by an associate of mine how I can justify the decision of the federal government to prorogue Parliament. She asked: "Does that decision not represent a disdain for the political process and a dictatorial attitude on the part of our Prime Minister?"

My answers were the following.

First, the political process begins and ends with the power of the electorate in Canada to choose their political representatives. To prorogue Parliament is to send Members of Parliament back to their home ridings. When back in their ridings those Members can meet much more frequently and extensively with their voting public than when they sit in the House. To send Members of Parliament back to their ridings is not anti-democratic.

Second, my personal view is that the pressures in the House prior to the decision to prorogue were not pressures that reflected well upon the political process. The contrarian ways among Parliamentarians these days were moving the Afghan detainee issue towards a witch-hunt that would be costly and acrimonious. The Canadian effort in Afghanistan deserves better than this.

In my view, which echoes what I read in some of our papers, there may be great merit in opening a debate about how Canada should use it powers (military, financial, political) in situations such as now found in Afghanistan. Similar situations may arise in Pakistan, in Yemen, or elsewhere. How should Canada expect to conduct itself and its operations in the kind of "warfare" we see more and more in the world today?

I did not get a sense, prior to Parliament being prorogued, that Members of Parliament would have been getting to that larger question if the Opposition attacks on the Government had continued. I hope Parliamentarians will turn their minds to the larger questions after they get back to their ridings and talk to their electorate.

Regarding the bills that died on the Order Paper, the fact is that the Opposition parties were not strong supporters of much of that legislation. Again, over the extra few weeks that the prorogation will provide, Members can check the pulse of their electorates and reaffirm where they stand individually and collectively on the business of the Government. Legislation which is already drafted. Those bills can move forward very quickly when Parliament resumes.

Finally, regarding the charge of "dictatorial" conduct, I reminded my associate that Mr. Harper is Prime Minister in a minority government situation.

To say that a Prime Minister can act dictatorially in a minority situation is to say a whole lot. It requires Opposition parties to support what a dictator may propose. One cannot be a dictator in Canada in a minority situation.

My concluding comment was that the "dictator" charge is part of the "we do not trust the Conservatives" concern.

Many people in this riding know what kind of man I am. They know that my lifelong approach reflects balance in almost everything that I do. They know that I respect Canada's traditions and reflect them in my own background and career.

I am a strong supporter of Canadian conservatism and I intend to become part of Mr. Harper's Government when the next election is held. You can be very confident that conservatives such as I can be fully trusted, I will talk back to the power centres in our party when it is necessary, and I will always serve Canada very well.

This was one of many letters I wrote to local and regional papers, most of which —like the one above—were published, some of which were not. All of them, however, went into the dossier from which I drew when I authored my speeches and wrote content for my website and Facebook page.

In print and in person, I always strived to represent as honestly as possible my own version of conservatism. During an appearance at the Ottawa University student Conservative association, I was welcomed by a group of about forty students who listened to my half-hour presentation. I gave the students my slant on what conservatism means: in short, "I can do it myself," but within a context of history, tradition, laws, and policies that empower all of us to the greatest extent possible.

When they asked me how and why I got involved in the political process, I used the opportunity to observe upon the importance of our being engaged in political discussion and political organization. But there was no follow-up debate or interrogation of my views. The students gave me a quick thank-you for my attendance and promptly turned their attention to making an endless list of technical amendments to their constitution, well led by an animated fellow who knew *Robert's Rules of Order* backward and forward. I slipped out of the room and headed home, more than a little disappointed by the disinterest in substantive debate.

You will remember I came into this business while reading Kershaw on politics in Germany at the time of Hitler's rise to power. Kershaw observed upon how Hitler's movement began in the beer halls, to which Nazi party workers and interested members of the public were invited to hear Hitler speak. Whereas Hitler convened his supporters over beer in order to bring democracy to an end, I wanted to make democracy in my area of the country work a little better. My grand idea was that democracy could be reborn. I wondered if the day would ever come when I would be part of an assembled group in a pub somewhere who got so excited that we all marched out and talked enthusiastically about politics to friends and neighbours. It would be revolutionary. I suggested to the EDA that we begin a series of town hall meetings where I would make myself available to talk with any and all citizens who cared to attend. I was eager to go public on the back of political discourse.

There never was any follow-up on the town hall idea. I found that getting people to talk about politics — whether university students, political staffers, or the average citizen — was very difficult. Drinks alone wouldn't do it! I had "come out" as a Conservative, but few were willing to enter into a public discourse about what really matters, or to debate with me the merits of a conservative orientation to politics in Canada.

Talking politics with their candidate was not high on the to-do list of EDA members or my top financial supporters either. At a meeting of the 400 Club, the one where the number referred to dollars contributed rather than the number of participants, I spoke enthusiastically about the need to begin a political dialogue within our community. I proposed that club members view themselves as the core group who would begin to meet among themselves and with friends and neighbours to discuss political issues and political directions. As candidate, and after being elected, I said, I would be pleased to join in their discussions and help change the passive political culture we have allowed to evolve.

The assembled members of the 400 Club had little time for my proposal. They saw themselves as part of my fundraising efforts, nothing more. One of the most dependable funders said, "Sir, frankly we don't care about talking politics with you. We are here because for a Conservative Party candidate to win in this riding, you need lots of money. We are here because you need money, and that's it."

Dr. Balaka, a thoughtful specialist in pediatrics who believed in the importance of the political process and who, I learned, could be counted upon to help me with financial contributions from time to time, had attended the meeting at my request. He offered a middle-of-the-road option: members are more likely to join the club and keep contributing, he said, if in return they get to meet with high-profile political people who are invited to address one or more of the political issues which are topical in the House of Commons or in the media.

I brought the meeting to a conclusion by subscribing to Dr. Balaka's proposal and by saying that — during an election — I would feel comfortable asking club members to pay an additional $400 to buttress the funds available at the start of the campaign. I received agreement about this, perhaps a bit hesitantly given, but I said a couple of times that my shyness about asking for money would not stop me from approaching 400 Club members when the writ was dropped. I said nothing more about political issues.

Instead of going public in person on the back of political discourse as I had hoped, I had to go public in the pursuit of money. While I was pleased to have made headway on my quest to secure funding for an eventual campaign, I regretted that politics remains — including for 400 Club members — a contest about money and numbers rather than a time for discussion, debate, and persuasion. The consensus appeared to be that the time for discussion would come, if at all, after I won the election. Only then would people be enthusiastic about hearing my political views.

Upon reflection, though I did not yet understand this at the time, even my most dependable supporters appreciated that the only political opinions that really mattered are those of the very few elected representatives who sit at the highest levels, namely cabinet ministers. Those few are in a position to get undertakings from party platforms and government policy statements implemented in laws and regulations. My EDA and I could always draw a crowd when events featured a member of the cabinet. Back bench members of parliament were not as big a draw. Folks like me, just starting out and highly likely to revert to ordinary citizenship after the next election, were perceived to have no more influence over platforms and policies than my supporters had themselves. Simply to talk among ourselves and learn... who had the time for that kind of stuff anyway?

In addition to the 400 Club, the EDA planned stand-alone fundraising events. One of these was a '50s/'60s dance, planned for January 2010. The venue was already booked when shocking news hit the airwaves: there had been a devastating earthquake in Haiti. All of Canada was saddened by the headlines. We in Ottawa–Vanier could not have it appear that the area Conservatives planned to fiddle while Rome (read "Haiti") burned. I was nevertheless asked by Guy, our fundraising chair, to agree with him that the dance should proceed. The problems were twofold. First, there was the problem of the association appearing to dance while Haiti went down the tubes. Since the previous CPC candidate in our riding was Haitian by birth, this would look especially bad and could even become grist for the mill for our main rival in the riding.

The second problem was that the dance, intended by the association to happen at the end of the month, should have been fully subscribed already. To sell tickets only two weeks before a scheduled event is surely a high-risk strategy. Guy told me, "Carol would not allow me to begin selling tickets until now!" Then he added, "Look, I booked the hall and the band two months ago. We're on the hook for the payments."

Our being in this position reflected our predicament as an association. It was blocked within itself. It was totally unable to deliver upon undertakings made by one association member because another member always had a better idea. Carol, the president, had dealt with this problem in what I learned would be her usual way. In her one-on-one meetings with Colin McSweeny, the CPC national association's representative responsible for EDAs in eastern Ontario, and with me, she sought to stop the planned event.

Stopping things was a habit of hers. She almost always offered useful alternatives, but forward momentum with the idea already in front of us would come to a halt. In this case she proposed that the dance be turned into a free event that encouraged those attending to donate toward the ongoing efforts in Haiti.

My advice to Carol, and separately to Guy, was to decide the future of the dance — and the association's response to the Haiti situation — in the context of a newly established executive committee within the structure of our EDA. Also, I advised again and again that the association should do nothing without first securing the support of Patrick Glémaud, the previous CPC candidate.

Patrick had been our candidate in the 2008 federal election. He had lost but had been expected to run again. He was well connected with operatives in the Conservative Party, including a former member of Parliament from Alberta and his wife, at that time a minister in the government — so much so that a couple of EDAs in the west had made his run possible by providing loans to compensate for our association's paltry fundraising efforts. Those loans became a challenge for me to help pay off after Patrick had resigned and my opportunity to run in his place had come.

On balance, after discussing a number of alternatives with Marie and taking note of the payments already made, I recommended to Guy that the dance continue — if he could get the numbers out — but that all profits be turned over to whichever group Patrick designated as the most worthy and/or useful in the eyes of his community. We also could offer non-financial assistance (babysitting for parents going to meetings to learn about developments in Haiti) or support families in our riding who had phone bills or travel costs to pay. Our support could go on for months rather than be one-time.

In the end, we cancelled the dance, not only because of public emotions or optics, but also because only seven tickets had been sold.

The seven tickets issue harkens back to what I have said about the weakness of Guy DesRoches in the fundraising role. Guy's approach was to fix the date, pick a place, commit to the entertainment and to the food, and then wait for the number of subscribers to the event build up. If only it could be so easy! There was no one around to help him, you see. He was acting like a manager, but one without any staff. We would end up making commitments without sufficient subscribers to cover even a portion of the already-sunk costs. And then there would be anger all round, directed at Guy, particularly from the EDA president and treasurer. I, for my part, would despair as I saw yet another opportunity to build up a cash reserve for an eventual campaign fall apart.

I believe it was out of necessity that I began to insert myself more and more into the fundraising business. I pressed upon my wife to open the door to our home to *cinq à septs* (wine and cheese events) and to dinner gatherings. I announced my intention to be available for chats about politics at public events or at a selected bar in the evenings, and so forth. As the bank account of the EDA began to grow, I began to presume an earned right to determine how the money should be spent. This presumption on my part raised tensions between me, Carol, and Ross.

In addition to public appearances, profile management, and fundraising, another activity that I had to get used to quickly was door-knocking. Door-knocking is the quintessential practice of electoral politics. Candidates often literally sprint from front door to front door, as televised on the evening news during elections. In my early days as candidate, before an election was called, I wanted to take my time with this. My association executive instructed me to pick that pace up. The number of doors knocked on mattered more, I was told, than the number of conversations. I would eventually conclude that this quintessential practice masks the deterioration in participatory politics.

I have a fundamental reluctance to impose myself into the privacy of other people. Once I got over this hurdle and engaged, however, I threw myself into the effort and often had some fun.

One afternoon we went out with teams of two, one team on each side of the street, with me hanging back. My role was to run up to individual homes whenever residents said they would like to see the candidate. But this did not happen very much. It seemed that all I would be doing was walking idly along the sidewalks, waiting for the calls that rarely came.

So I lost patience within a half-hour and began going door to door on my own. When one of the two teams knocked on doors, they would sometimes be told, "But Mr. Westland has already been here!"

One of the main things I learned from this exercise is the great importance — for the candidate, if not for EDAs — of meeting as many potential voters as possible. Door-knocking is one way to do this, even though a typical evening round can bring you to only a few dozen residences if your purpose is meaningful dialogue. I found I had a pretty good way with people when I engaged in a simple meet-and-greet. I was able to consider observations they made and relate their observations to my own orientation as a conservative. I knew the party positions well enough to bring CPC positions into a discussion as well.

I also learned that my goal to promote political discussion could — again, if only on a small scale — be achieved. At one home, the man of the house was clearly uninterested in hearing what I might have to say. I found a way to kid him a bit, however, and his son happened to be sitting on the doorstep. So I sold my line to the son.

The father then told his son that he — the son — would vote as Father told him to. It was intended as a joke and received as one. But as I was leaving the property, I overheard the son asking his Dad, "Dad, who's the MP for this area, and why do you prefer him to that guy?" I suspect the political discussion that followed was the first round of political exchange those two ever had. The time I had spent in the discussion, of course, would at best have netted me one vote in the upcoming election. I needed about twenty thousand votes to win.

On another round of door-knocking, Marie drove the Jeep so that we would have a car to ferry me from one home to another if my two teams of supporters (two people each) got too far apart. Plastered along the sides of the jeep were the coordinates for my website… a stand-out feature which Marie did not enjoy very much. I realized, however, that there was great merit in my walking down Ottawa–Vanier streets with nothing more than the Jeep behind me, my name and email address emblazoned on the doors and loud music blaring from the radio. We could revert back, I mused, to the political bandwagon days of John A. Macdonald. Marie's preference for quiet and private strolls through our neighbourhood was being displaced by very public displays of my intentions.

I would say it took about six months of active politicking (and there would be thirteen to go) before I had a truly realistic sense of what I had gotten myself into. Standing out in front to represent the political initiatives of my party and to champion my own merits as a potential member of Parliament became my new normal. Holding back, waiting to be called, responding to whatever was incoming, were no longer options. I had to take the initiative or else sit at home and twiddle my thumbs until an election was called.

The remarkable fact is that my enjoyment of what I needed to do did not let up. My actions had been provoked by a felt imperative to not look the fool when I emerged from the other end of this gauntlet. Being proud, being public, being bold — those were the only options. Once I had gotten my measure of this crazy business, I was able to park my private self at home and revel in the public experience.

My sacrifice of privacy continued to grow throughout the nineteen months. Some of that sacrifice was already behind me, such as the privacy I had lost when I stepped out of the closet in my Liberal riding with a jacket featuring the CPC logo and colours. Some of the sacrifice happened every day when I stepped in front of my EDA's failing money-raising ventures and pleaded one on one with neighbours and local business leaders for personal and financial support. My cover was lost when letters began to appear in local and regional newspapers, letters in which I explained my support for the Conservative government's unpopular decisions. To search my name on the Internet was to land upon my smiling face, shaking hands with Prime Minister Harper. With each initiative, my association with the Conservative Party of Canada—once always private—was publicly reaffirmed.

A number of tests still lay in front of me, such as the need to collapse my RRSPs in order to find the money to keep going, such as the sacrifice of the time and care it takes to be a good husband for my wife and father to my adult children. Marie, more than I, would line the long and growing list of sacrifices up against the dubious merits of a role, that of designated candidate, that paid absolutely nothing and held out only the faintest of promise that there would be a reward at its end. It made for heated debate between us many a time, too often over morning coffee.

CHAPTER 3.

THE TEST OF VALUES

Whether the candidate is consciously aware of it or not, running for public office in a democratic country places that candidate smack dab in the middle of an engagement with democratic values and principles. The novice is more likely to know this than the politico. A party's chosen star candidate, even if a novice, may be too caught up in his or her own lustre to take stock of what this means.

At the highest level, it means fundamental beliefs are in play regarding liberty, equality of opportunity, and justice for all. Constitutional principles unique to democratic systems such as rule of law, separation of powers, and individual rights are engaged as well. The values and principles which underlie the success of democratic systems are tied down not by institutions and established processes (though these certainly help) but by what elected members of federal and provincial parliaments individually and collectively believe. Democracy is maintained by the courage of those people to act on their beliefs.

I brought four imperatives into the game with me. And I stuck with — indeed, reinforced — them as I got further in.

First, I believe that a candidate for public office must be who and what he or she seems to be. I had no intention to hide behind the political party I represented. After the writ dropped, and therefore during the campaign, there was only one occasion on which I allowed the CPC to stand in front of me, and that was with a large advertisement in regional papers that screamed out three or four core messages. I regret doing that.

Second, I am of the view that equality and justice for all begin with a candidate's belief that every voter and every group of voters matters. It is not good enough to go after the low-hanging fruit, namely, the polls where the majority of voters are most likely to cast ballots in your favour. To ignore or even discourage voters who you know will vote for other parties is wrong.

Third, respect for voters means moving beyond simple slogans. When a door is opened or contact on the street is made, the candidate must be prepared to take the time to engage a citizen in dialogue over the issues. Whenever I was asked where I or the CPC stood, I always gave whatever time it took to provide detailed explanations of my personal views or party platforms.

Fourth, truth and transparency go hand in hand. Whenever I was asked about my position on an issue that I knew attracted a large number of voters to the CPC in my riding (right to life, for example) or on an issue that turned off a great many others (easing of gun control), I would begin with an accurate statement of where my party stood. I would then engage in a give-and-take about that stance, and, if my personal view differed from that of my party, I would say why my having that view did not compromise my determination, if elected, to stand with the Conservatives in the House of Commons.

The test of values happens at each and every door, and with each and every interpersonal contact that a candidate makes.

Whether and how one worships God, for example, is an issue that CPC candidates in particular must wrestle with. The sitting CPC member of Parliament in a neighbouring riding advised me to go to a church every Sunday, perhaps twice on a Sunday and again on other days of the week, to show off my piety and to meet parishioners. My association leaders countered by saying that my attending services did not matter. What I needed to do, the EDA advised, was stand outside the doors of churches in our riding when services ended so that I could meet departing faithful on their way home. One of our board members offered a schedule of different churches and other religious institutions in Ottawa–Vanier and showed how I could run from one closing service to another and chalk up as many as four in a day.

I could not do any of that. I was not a regular at the church my family attended on special occasions, and I would not pretend otherwise. But I said that I was open to joining EDA members at their respective places of worship if asked. I was asked a number of times, most frequently by new Canadians of Congolese, Sudanese, and Haitian origin. In their churches I took my turn following the priest or pastor to talk about God and politics.

I was exhorted to drop in at a mosque or two. I had seen many politicians alter their normal dress to render it appropriate for entry into those places of worship. More importantly, I had noted the absence of their wives. I was not interested.

The democratic values of liberty and rule of law were engaged when I spoke to new Canadians, such as those from Sudan who were working with contacts in North Africa to achieve a political separation between the northern and southern parts of their home country. At a gathering of a few hundred Sudanese Canadians, following speakers coming from many walks of life and professions, I was the only one who addressed those attending as "fellow Canadians." There was loud applause in answer to my greeting. I then spoke about Quebec within Canada and reflected upon what I had learned during my time with the Task Force on Canadian Unity.

"Your eye," I said, "should also be upon the country we are all now a part of. Your eye should be upon Canada. What have we learned as Canadians about political divides that threaten the breakup of a country? You are uniquely placed to bring lessons learned in Canada to what is transpiring back in Sudan. You are picking up knowledge from your family and friends in Sudan about what happens when a separation actually occurs. I hope that lesson never has relevance in Canada, but if it does, your advice will be listened to."

My valuing of equality between men and women was tested when I was going door to door in a neighbourhood where there is a high concentration of new Canadians from countries in the Middle East. Two women, clearly very frightened, came up to me on the boulevard between rows of social housing. In severely broken English, they described limitations placed on their activities by the men around them, and I could see a number of those men glaring at the three of us. The women asked me to please remember them if I was ever in a position to help. These were moments when I appreciated the awesome responsibility falling on the shoulders of elected members of Parliament if they take their responsibilities seriously. Successful candidates cannot rest until women such as these have a better chance to pursue employment opportunities for themselves, and to succeed.

Most of us have been encouraged by the image of sprinting candidates throwing leaflets around to believe that door-knocking such as I was doing in the Beauséjour sector of my riding is the lifeblood of electoral politics. Winning an election, successful candidates unanimously say, is dependent above all upon an aggressive door-to-door campaign.

I expected this traditional activity to be a surefire way to implement the test of values. But take a closer look.

If you want meaningful contact with a voter at the door or in the street, you should realistically allot five minutes to each engagement: three to talk, two to get to the next person. Given that direct voter contact (or DVC, as it is called in the business) is not welcomed by most residents between elections, you have five weeks to get this done. At five minutes per meeting, twelve contacts per hour, and sixty people per day — assuming five hours between eating, family, projects, and so on — you can have meaningful contact with 2,100 voters in the course of an election if you do almost nothing else. If you are running in an urban riding such as Ottawa–Vanier, there are likely to be approximately 60,000 registered voters in total.

It always bothered me when I heard other candidates, especially those who had won their elections, say they had knocked "on every door in my riding." In the most recent municipal election in Ottawa, I followed the track of two candidates in particular, because I knew them personally. One affirmed with pride that he had already knocked on 14,000 doors before the municipal election began (the period during which most doors stay firmly shut to the nuisance of politicians). The other, much more proudly still, declared that he and his team had knocked on 27,000 doors… twice! What utter nonsense.

Such absurd claims, and the image of democracy in action when the television shows candidates running from door to door, stands for me as a profound insult to the values I have just outlined. I have said that we candidates participate in a sham when we do this. We obfuscate the truth of what long ago began to happen to democracy on the ground, likely when the number of eligible voters began to grow from the hundreds to the thousands. By so fervently playing "let's pretend" we stand between the truth and the imperative to change how things work.

Nonetheless, at this juncture in the democratic lives of Canadians, campaigning door to door is an essential rite of passage. It may not make much difference, it may even help to perpetuate a myth, but to not do it would be viewed by the public as an affront.

So since you *must* go door-knocking, if you want to do a thorough job of it you had better get walking! You could get a jump on the election, of course. Once you are the candidate, you can begin right away. But you won't legally be allowed through the locked front doors of any high-rise buildings. Also, to knock on doors out of season (when an election has not yet been called) is to invite rejection by the residents you have disturbed. People who do not like your party can actually get quite angry.

Even so, if you persist, you will often find that the initial reluctance when the door opens gives way fairly quickly to a sense of welcome. You may even be struck by the pleasure that some folks express when they learn about your purpose. In those few cases, the desire to talk about politics and to compare notes about recent political events can become hour-long sessions if you allow it. This isn't good for numbers. You cannot make personal contact with 14,000 voters (let alone 27,000 voters, twice) if you do this.

Before the writ drops a door-knocking candidate is often on his or her own. I was occasionally lucky enough to have help — co-knockers who get the resident to the door in the next house over while you wrap up with their neighbours. Maybe this will help you shave thirty seconds off each interaction. That's useful.

However, what is more likely is that those helpers will hustle you along and pressure you to behave quite differently at the door than, if you are at all like me, you would like to. The priority of your helpers, who between elections are sure to be committed party workers, will be to ask the same questions over and over. Questions such as "How many voters live in this house?" "How many will be voting Conservative in the next election?" "Will you pay $10 for a party membership?" "Do you think you will need assistance getting to the voting booth?" and so on. None of these questions has anything to do with values.

The doors are usually slammed in a candidate's face before the second question can be asked anyway, but still your helpers will urge you to play along. This is because of what is in the instructions from the party's head office. These are the rules of direct voter contact. These are your voter-identification (Voter ID) questions. Your party and your helpers want you to be a political census taker.

Gathering data on the voting intentions of residents, in my view, is a job that should be done between elections by the association itself, not at the cost of a candidate's public image and especially not during the campaign. But for EDA executive members and party workers, the data of politics have become extremely important. If there is more work to be done after a candidate has been designated, gathering data is the number-one concern.

The science of electoral politics is nothing more than a few programs which aim to base the electoral strategy of political parties and their candidates upon hard numbers. Rigour has supposedly entered into the system. At least that is what must be pretended by everyone who wants to be taken seriously these days.

The programs in question have become familiar to Canadians in recent years. Between elections, political parties are increasingly oriented toward DVC. One of the driving purposes of DVC is to obtain information from residents with regard to their voting habits and intentions. In the Conservative Party of Canada, we used walk sheets, which identified homes and home owners in all corners of the riding. When we knocked on doors or placed telephone calls, we were supposed to ask if the resident intended to vote Conservative in the next election. The possible answers were "most definitely," "unsure," or "definitely not." These data were then entered into a central database known as the Constituency Information Management System (CIMS).

In my riding, the Liberal Party of Canada develops and maintains similar records on voters. In an inquiry launched against the sitting member of Parliament for allegedly making his Liberal list available to a friend running at the municipal level, the monetary value of the Liberal list was said to be well over a municipal candidate's allowed maximum expenditure.

The idea behind these data is that during the election candidates and their offices will work the telephones to get out the vote (GOTV). If it takes 20,000 votes to win an election, as was the case in my riding, and if the CIMS data input by my EDA was accurate for as many as half of these, we could in principle increase our chances of winning by making direct voter contact during the election and helping to deliver 10,000 known supporters to the polls on voting day. On the other hand, if our data are wrong or if we call people who have changed their minds, it could also mean that we piss people off.

The truth is, this stuff is mostly nonsense. When federal and provincial governments develop legislation to apply limits to robo-calls, it is at best symbolic. Those programs are symptoms of something bad that is happening to electoral politics in Canada. We are overly focused upon the symptoms.

It is physically impossible to obtain and maintain accurate data on the scale that would be required to make that data meaningful. To make telephone calls or to visit the 60,000 voters in Ottawa–Vanier would require that a well-oiled EDA make DVC a regular and disciplined activity. To knock on doors and record information on the residents of even a hundred houses, if you allow for ten minutes per house to ask all those stupid questions and write down the answers, would take three five-hour days for one person. To turn this into a thousand homes would increase the draw in human resources by a factor of ten. In my riding, you would need to increase the requirement by an additional factor of sixty or so. And then you move into the high-rises. Oh yes — the high-rises must wait until an election is called, because you cannot legally demand access to them until the writ drops.

The trouble is that electoral district associations which support opposition candidates operate on the edge of solvency. They can cover their costs, but many must struggle to keep a net balance so that their candidate can start a campaign with money in the bank. They do not have the money to hire dependable telephone- or Internet-based census takers. The available staff is counted in the tens, not the hundreds, of volunteers. The resources required to create truly effective information banks far, far exceeds the capacity of most, if not all, EDAs in the country.

This is one reason why party workers stoop to cheating. Everyone knows what the target is (all questions honestly answered, for each house on each walk sheet). Everyone knows what the standard is (accurate answers for all residents of voting age in each house). Everyone knows that achieving the target and meeting the standard is impossible. Not a single resident in not a single home whose door opened to me in my riding had either the will or the patience to answer more than one of the questions. Under such conditions, people cheat.

One way to cheat is to run through neighbourhoods as quickly as one can and then make up the data. In my case, what I learned on my rounds when knocking on doors hardly ever matched the paltry bits of information in our CIMS. I could not even trust the data well enough to wish the best to a Mister or Miss X if he or she was a "supporter." Once bitten, twice shy. After learning that a person whose views had allegedly been solicited the week before had actually been dead for many years, I stopped using the data altogether.

I learned from newspaper reports about a riding in Guelph that another way to cheat is to set aside one's own DVC data, claim to represent one of the other political parties, and place random telephone calls to people not on your own lists. In those random calls you say you belong to the same political party as they do and you say nasty things. On election day, you send them to the wrong place to vote. An extremely aggressive effort of this kind might affect a hundred or so votes. In my riding a candidate needed 20,000 votes to win.

The most terrible cheat is upon the political process itself. The logic of the DVC programs lends itself to a presumption of — even a will for — low voter turnout. If one party believes it has accurate data on 10,000 supporters, for example, a highly desired outcome on voting day is for that party's supporters to be driven to the polls (figuratively and sometimes literally) and for everyone else to stay home. For a disciplined political party whose EDAs have done their jobs between elections, the wet dream is that voter turnout will be so low that their own GOTV program can make all the difference. If this takes misdirecting a few voters in hostile areas of town so that they give up and return home, so be it. Cheating is a direct consequence of impossible logic, impossible targets, and impossible standards.

The "science" of electoral politics usually makes little difference in the overall result on voting day. Senior people in my party have observed that these programs can be influential only in ridings where the election is extremely close, so that a few dozen votes can determine the outcome. These programs do, however, have a number of nefarious consequences for democracy.

The intended work of EDAs — already compromised by limited funds and the capacities of its members — is distorted. First, because EDAs cannot possibly do what the DVC programs expect of them, they do almost nothing instead. They are not encouraged to promote alternative activities such as the hosting of public discussions and debate. Second, the drive for hard numbers has reduced the interest in dialogue to almost nothing. Third, because the targets and standards of DVC programs are ridiculously impossible to meet, party workers do what humans do under such circumstances: they cheat. After they have quietly given up on the idea that their support base can become known "scientifically," some political party workers focus instead upon discouraging the support base of other parties. A fourth unhappy consequence is that one finds among EDA volunteers, and even in the ranks of successful politicians, a large and growing number of people who admit to being cynical about the political process, even if they have been handsomely rewarded by the outcome of it.

The worst consequence of the science of politics has been alluded to already: candidates and what they may believe about democracy are no longer seen as being very relevant. When the primary purpose for direct voter contact becomes the gathering of information about political orientation, and when the driving objective during a campaign is to get out the vote — but only of those voters you know for sure will vote for your own party — the role of the candidate greatly changes. The talent of persuasion, one that the novice candidate developed to high degree in his or her business or public-sector career, is totally out of vogue.

The candidate still says "Vote for me." There are a lot of things the candidate still does that are vestiges of campaigns generations ago. But the candidate has now become a high-energy tool to be used by EDAs between elections and by campaign managers during elections to update data banks. The science of politics is meant to avoid the distortion in central messaging that sets in when candidates talk politics. They risk polluting "scientific methods" and results.

But it's not "science" at all. It is more like crowdsourcing for votes. The gap between the appeal for votes and voting itself is filled with slogans and jargon rather than with discussions about values and with persuasion.

Those crazy programs have become a target for media critics who deplore the current condition of democracy in our country. But the programs are not the issue: lack of participation is the issue.

The programs have been developed to take advantage of, and feed into, declining participation rates. In their cynicism, the programs may indeed be making things worse. But participation does not happen anymore between elections. There is no time during the election itself to make up for this.

Before leaving the topic of door-knocking and DVC, I want to return to the one aspect of direct voter contact activities that *does* matter.

Even though a candidate who is honest with himself or herself will know that personal contact with voters can be achieved with only a very small percentage of those who will be voting, to look a couple of thousand residents in the eye and to expose yourself to a dialogue that may sometimes go directly to difficult issues and to personal values, is to submit yourself to a meaningful test of who you are and what you stand for. Door-knocking and direct voter contact in the lobby of high-rises, at the front doors of private homes, in businesses' reception areas, or in public settings like restaurants mean very little in terms of winning or losing. But they can mean a heck of a lot in terms of what the candidate learns about himself or herself. There is always the risk, furthermore, that a candidate with the wrong values gets exposed.

Reasonably competitive and fair elections is a collectively held value that lies at the heart of democracies like ours. In Ottawa–Vanier, the realization of this value has become impossible.

The Liberal Party of Canada has held this seat ever since the riding was created. The seat was considered a fiefdom by Liberal incumbents and their followers to the extent that the local Liberal member of Parliament asked a mutual acquaintance why someone of my professional stature would bother running in "his" jurisdiction. I answered that effective democracies require citizens of my stature to compete for public office if the opportunity to do so comes our way.

The MP representing Ottawa–Vanier is a man named Mauril Bélanger. I learned to rather like the fellow, but I deeply resented his — and his party's — presumptions with regard to the riding. They had left the assumption of a competitive political process behind generations ago. Had Mauril been a man with gravitas and charisma, I might have been persuaded that something other than a drift away from democratic principles was in play. But he was not such a man.

Mr. Bélanger was an experienced politico, well into his middle years — a career politician. Like so many others in this class, his curriculum vitae continues to include roles like volunteer while in high school and student leader while in university, always with the Liberals. The CV of a novice like me focuses upon professional contributions and often displays a wide range of these.

Our having been class president or football quarterback in high school was dropped decades ago.

When Mr. Bélanger was first presented to the House of Commons, replacing the Liberal politician on whose staff he had been an advisor, he observed that he was not the most attractive of men. On that point I disagreed with him. He had an attractive way about him. But he could also turn his dark look and large frame into a menacing presence. Given that he had wielded influence, and sometimes even power, in Ottawa–Vanier for sixteen years before I stood up against him, I knew that persuading those who habitually voted for him to vote for me would be difficult. I learned that there were residents in the riding who were afraid of what the loss of his influence could mean if they stood publicly with me.

That said, Mr. Bélanger's numbers had been going down in each federal election previous to mine, from a high of 60% of all those voting when he started out to hovering just under 50% in the 2006 and 2008 elections. In the 2011 election, he would fall down to under 40%. I like to think that my effort contributed 5% to his slide. The NDP candidate, boosted by the Jack Layton effect, took away another 5%. Jack Layton, the leader of the NDP, had endeared himself especially to francophone voters in Canada because of his courage in the face of a cancer that would kill him. He handled himself with humour and aplomb, and with fluency in French. The French-speaking population in Vanier and parts of Orleans loved him.

In spite of the odds against me, I wanted to acquit myself honourably. I spoke up loudly, forcefully, and repeatedly. I read widely about issues that might impact upon my riding, including how the publicly lamented government purchase of F35 jets might play out among small industries in the Ottawa–Vanier technology sector.

At the door of those who affirmed "We always vote Liberal in this house," there sometimes (rarely) were serious issues raised, but there was usually a smile and a 'thank-you' by the time I walked away. At at least a couple of homes, I felt I achieved "conversion," which is something that the DVC and Voter ID logic has no interest in.

In fact, I took the logic of the words "direct voter contact" as far as possible into the realm of real human interaction as I could.

I worried that the residents' disinclination to talk politics might be a problem linked entirely to me personally or to the party I represented. That is one of the reasons I was very interested in what Mauril Bélanger might be accomplishing at the "coffees" he held from time to time across the riding. I had my team attend three of those events. The attendance was in the twos and threes, plus my delegates and a number of folks from the sitting MP's office. The talk during his coffees, following a fifteen-minute monologue that repeated the contents of his latest newsletter, was almost exclusively about immigration issues. The issues were brought to him at the meeting by the two or three members of the public. Mr. Bélanger, if his goal had been to keep political discourse alive in Ottawa–Vanier between elections, was having no more success than I was. In my diary I wrote, "If this is the best that a backbench member of Parliament can do, why would anyone want the job?"

One cold February morning in 2010, I met with Gene Pierce, a member of the executive of our EDA, at a ballpark on the edge of Beacon Hill, a suburb in my riding. Gene, a tall man in his late fifties with a left-leaning gait when striding door to door, had been a member of the selections committee which had approved me as candidate. He was a bit of an oddball in the Ottawa–Vanier political process because, though an official resident of Canada, he was still a citizen of the United States. He was not eligible to vote in Canada. He had been with the Embassy of the United States in Ottawa before leaving that country's public service and deciding to remain in Canada. He certainly knew our riding very well. He was just as familiar with the back alleys in the poorest areas of town as he was with the pleasant and tree-lined lanes of Rockcliffe.

Gene knew all the schools; he knew where the churches and the mosques were; he could talk knowingly about the different cultures in the riding and who lived where. He knew Ottawa–Vanier like the back of his hand. He drove me hither and yon for the better part of two weeks. We would stop for coffee along the way, and from time to time we stopped to knock on the door of a "supporter" whom he had come to know over his period with the association. With regard to Gene, I had a lot to be grateful for. Yet I never really warmed to him. I truly regret that. A better feeling may have had me be more open-minded about the directions he was trying to set.

Gene was devoted to the science of politics. The Voter ID programs were more than a set of numbers-based activities to him. He strived to be professionally involved at the party HQ level in making those programs work. At one point, through my firm, he hoped to win consulting contracts in this specialization.

That morning at the ballpark, his goal was to convince me to fill in our Beacon Hill walk sheets with numbers. My goal, on the other hand, was to engage residents in substantive discussion and not bother them with a probe into their personal voting intentions.

I elaborated upon my concerns regarding the association's performance and upon my view that those programs — even if we had the dozens of volunteers and thousands of dollars needed to implement them — were more alienating of potential voters than positive in their result. I wanted my campaign plan to be affordable. To pull together the material needed to help me engage meaningfully with riding residents on my terms would already cost a bundle. We did not have the money to implement Voter ID programs as well.

In answer, Gene placed before me all the arguments and tactics I had been hearing from established CPC interests for the last four months. Gene believed that the DVC programs were the way to go, notwithstanding what I could point to as clear evidence that it was too late for Voter ID to be made accurate; and that it was too expensive to design and implement GOTV in our riding. When I challenged him to show why — with all of its failings to date — he believed the association could help him achieve his "higher order" of election activities and expenses, Gene had no answer. He apologized for the association's poor performance to date and affirmed — as others had every step of the way — that things would get better soon.

In the end I assessed that Gene would help deliver the kind of campaign I wanted to see delivered as long as, in return, I left the door open to the contemporary "science" of electioneering and to the related costs (all much higher). I made it clear that the delivery of the necessary additional resources, both people and money, would have to be done by someone other than me. My qualified concession kept open the door to friendship and cooperation between us for a few more months. Gene would eventually become co-manager of my campaign on an interim basis, and then he would quit.

Around the same time that winter, I spent an evening with Guy DesRoches and a person who worked for the Manning Institute, a Conservative think tank. Fraser Mansbridge was a leading light, though only twenty-three, because his disciplined application of Conservative Party election techniques appeared to have closed impossible distances between Liberals and Conservatives in a couple of Ontario ridings, especially in Kingston.

Fraser elaborated upon the approach and the work required to implement the Voter ID election tool, GOTV, direct voter contact, and other such "programs."

At one point during his elaboration of these programs, I asked Fraser, "Do you find yourself getting cynical about the political process?"

His answer was quick: "Yes."

Two beers later he agreed with me that there will always be a place for old-time politics (he used the words "preaching and converting"). But old-time politics, he reaffirmed, are no longer associated by political party operatives with winning.

I certainly wanted to be a winner.

In the summer, World Cup fever had seized the city and soccer fans across the globe. I invited my son Kees, who was studying at McGill at the time, to come watch the final match, between Spain and the Netherlands, with me. We met for the game at a Portuguese festival taking place in my riding. It would be good to spend some quality time with my eldest son, and also good for my image. The number of people at the annual festival easily topped five hundred.

A supporter of mine was a small business owner in the riding and also a leader in the Portuguese community. The suggestion that I attend the festival to see the game had come from him.

When we arrived at the festival, however, I felt I had made a wrong decision. I should have chosen a smaller audience. Kees and I could have watched the game at the Café Caco, a restaurant specializing in Portuguese food, where the large TV screen was always tuned to a soccer game. The festival was too large a venue for me. I was lost in this place. But my rule of thumb had become "Do not refuse invitations!"

During the game Kees and I sat side by side in our orange apparel (my hat, his jersey). We were at the very front of the crowd, so we were definitely noticed. And that was the point! No one else from the campaign team was there.

To my astonishment, when the overtime halves began —the immensely exciting game had ended nil–nil — the festival organizers turned the television off. They shifted us spectators outdoors to watch a trampoline display. While Kees and I had become absorbed by what might be the fate of the Dutch team, given my own origins in that country, I had a rude awakening. The Portuguese people at the festival cared not one whit about the fate of Spain or Holland. Portugal had long been out of the running. So Kees and I raced off to watch the end of the game at home.

Holland lost. I was pleased that I had not had to bow out of the Portuguese embrace with a sense of loss hanging in the air. I did not want my image to be associated with a losing team.

Winning matters.

But the desire to win is not a democratic value. The desire to win is inculcated into the minds of many children by parents and teachers who oversee play and sports. The sitting MP in my riding, on our way into a studio inside the headquarters of our largest regional newspaper, beat his fists into the air and stamped his feet. "Running," he said to me, "is rather like a boxing match." He wondered if I was in it to win. If you are a novice candidate, you will learn that your competitive drive will shift into a higher gear with each challenge that is met and overcome.

Long after my run for public office was over, in early January 2014, I read an article in the regional paper, *The Ottawa Citizen*. In that article the political analyst Andrew Potter, editor-in-chief of the paper, wrote that there are two categories of political perspective: that of the cynical and that of the naive. The cynics see politics as a technical construct in which the goal is to secure power for a privileged group. For the cynics, the primacy of "programs" like Voter ID and GOTV makes tremendous sense. They look for discipline among those who stand for the party in a general election. Candidates are required to reaffirm policy content which has been geared to the number of votes required to win. Discipline in a candidate matters a whole lot more than intelligence.

The naive people are those who still want to believe that the individual candidate and personal values matter. They believe that the candidate who wins an election will be the one who corrals among a riding's residents the greatest possible consensus about important issues. The winning candidates then assemble in the House of Commons and debate among themselves what policies would respond best to the preferences expressed in each of the more than three hundred ridings across the country.

I have learned that party activists, like Fraser Mansbridge, are mostly cynics. For them, the kind of politics still imagined by the naive ones, like me, died a long time ago.

In late 2010, at a point in my candidacy when changing horses was a bad idea, both my interim campaign team manager and my co-manager parted company from me. We had experienced a crescendo in the values-based argument among us. The break came because of my refusal to go the route of the so-called science of politics. The election would be called only four months later.

The end between me and my leadership duo of Guy DesRoches and Gene Pierce came on November 25, at a meeting where I had pleaded that we organize to make a concerted effort to have a couple of hundred residents agree to endorse me as a candidate for public office — a legal requirement for running — and also undertake to have a lawn sign posted on their properties immediately after the writ fell. I wanted us to talk to those residents, over the telephone or in person, to let them know who I was and what my thoughts were about riding issues. I said I would be pleased to lean on the growing number of volunteers signed up to be campaign team workers in order to accomplish those goals.

Guy and Gene demurred. The meeting would be used to step up our effort to gather information required by the party's CIMS, they insisted, and I reluctantly agreed. But I agreed on condition that the volunteers used to get this done would be EDA members, not campaign team volunteers. "None of my campaign team members," I pointed out, "have any interest in doing the work of the EDA."

Not a single EDA volunteer showed up at the meeting. Gene nevertheless opened the discussion by laying out those offensive (to my eyes) walk sheets. The two campaign team volunteers who had showed up to "watch and learn" said they had no interest in the science of politics and walked away. Guy stormed out and Gene quit the next day.

I confronted the tension between a values-based approach to politics and a numbers-based approach only one more time after this. During the election itself, a young fellow who had joined my team from an MP's office on the Hill had set the stage for a telephone blitz, requiring a bank of two dozen or more telephones to be installed in my campaign office, for the purpose of confirming voting intentions and getting out the vote of those who said they would be voting Conservative. We almost came to blows. The blitz did not happen, and that young fellow left the building in a major hurry.

The last supper I shared with Guy and Gene had happened at my home only two months before. Marie had prepared everything, and my two team leaders (as they then still were) attended with their wives. Discussion among us before dinner, during the meal, and over coffee afterward was wide-ranging — serious for the most part, but great fun. Our topics were all political. Toward the end of the evening, Guy exclaimed with enthusiasm, "You know, this is why I went into politics. This is what I always wanted. This is the first time since I stepped into the political process almost a decade ago that I have spent an evening talking about politics with anyone other than my wife."

CHAPTER 4.

THE TEST OF COMMITMENT

The test of commitment is a matter of resources. What resources are called upon during a candidate's run for public office? What will does the candidate have to commit those resources and to leave them committed throughout the journey? Why is the demand placed upon a novice candidate so much greater than that placed upon a politico? Why would an "ordinary citizen," a person who has not devoted his or her life to politics, run the gauntlet if the test of commitment were known to be as great as it is?

The resources called upon include reputation, interpersonal relationships (family, friends, professional colleagues), organizational skills, and money. Already in the test of privacy and the test of values, the issues of reputation and interpersonal relations have been partially addressed.

I had not expected the test of commitment to be as severe as it was with respect to organizational skills and money because I had expected my electoral district association to have those two political imperatives well in hand. Let's talk first about the money. I will do this in a general way, and then I will take a look into my own pocketbook.

Upon my being nominated, my association told me that it is one of the tasks of a candidate to impress upon supporters in their riding the importance of participating in fundraising events. The maximum contribution allowed for an individual in a calendar year is now $1,500.00. It is the candidate's job to have his or her total cost shared among as many contributing people as possible. In the chapter on the test of privacy, I observed that I had thought this was the association's job.

Successive governments in Canada, at all levels, have turned their minds to the affordability of public life. The tax regime in Canada greatly reduces the financial burden on citizens who make such contributions to the cause of candidates, but it is still going to be difficult to convince people to part with their money. That is why it is going to cost a lot of your own money as well, quite likely in the six figures.

For starters, there are costs in the pre-nomination phase that must be borne before tax regulations even apply. It begins with lunches and dinners to which you invite family and friends so that your explaining and, if need be, your apologizing can begin.

To these initial expenses are added the receptions at your home where you begin to speak publicly about your intentions and your plans. To register as a candidate in a nomination convention costs at least a thousand dollars, often more, and while you may get some or all of that amount back from your party headquarters one day, the amount must first be paid out of pocket. You will learn what is eligible for reimbursement by the party and what is not. You will learn the true cost of postage when hundreds of letters are sent out. You will be amazed at how much pizza your volunteers will eat in one evening.

The more you get into this, the more you commiserate with other first-time candidates about the financial commitment. Municipal candidates need money and provincial candidates need money, and candidates at all levels build teams of supporters whose assistance and votes might one day make a great difference in your own campaign. So you contribute to the efforts of those other first-time candidates who impress you as individuals, regardless of party. In this domain of giving, the amounts that make a difference are in the order of hundreds of dollars.

You hope that the return one day will be measured in the number of volunteers who join your campaign after those municipal or provincial elections are over.

The further you move into the public sphere as a candidate, the faster your expenses begin to grow. The hits come in amounts from $20 to $200, and the hits keep coming. If you hope for votes from the owner of a business you are visiting, you can hardly leave without buying something. You cannot stop by an organization which promotes important social causes without making a donation. You cannot go to a community event which raises money for the homeless without money in your pocket. Having said that, keep in mind that politicos will not feel the same compulsion.

The younger ones have been in the business of politics for most of their short lives, as staffers in political office. Many appear to be just out of their teens. They have no money. Picking up the tab has not yet become a habit. You, the novice candidate, have a solid background and a bank account, and you have a set of manners to match. You pay your own way. You may not be getting anything back in return for your donation or contribution, but you can't imagine not making it. The older, successful politicos — the career politicians — pay their way with promises here and there to lever public funds. Deductible office donations are also an option. Those men and women earn an impressive salary while doing the same things that you, the novice, must do at your own expense.

Unlike the politicos, both young and old, politics is not your job. As you develop your public life, you will have less time and soon no time to earn money either from a salary or through your own business. You will learn that you must devote yourself full-time to being a candidate if you want to live up to your own expectations for yourself. Running for public office is an expensive business for people like you and me. For the politicos, not so much.

Fundraising events hosted by your EDA will not make much

difference for your bottom line. EDA events are attended in small numbers, and many of those attending are board and executive members who usually expect to participate for free because of everything else they are doing. I learned that an event that pays for itself is already a success; to raise a profit is amazing.

Politics is an expensive business. If you are considering throwing your name into the ring, take the time to review your financial position. Ensure that your spouse or partner is on side. You are certain to take a major hit on your pocketbook. Your financial commitment will be tested again and again, each time at a higher order of magnitude.

After just a few years in office, sitting MPs will have benefited from their positions in a number of ways. Elections Canada returns show that the incumbent in my riding could afford to raise 70% less money from personal contributions than I yet still spend almost twice as much because of money and material already parked with his EDA. He did not need to make a personal loan to his campaign. He did not need to use his own money to help out selected residents and local businesses: he could promise to leverage public funds already set aside in government programs.

The visibility of MPs in their ridings begins with their names emblazoned upon the signs outside their riding offices, paid for by taxpayers. They have been able to maintain a team of office staff who, when the time comes, are happy to work without pay for the five weeks it will take to win another campaign. As you equip yourself for your run, and as you discover the price tags on all the necessary gear, you will realize that you are an amateur running against a professional.

While working in the side yard one early-spring morning after I had been acclaimed as the candidate, my neighbour across the street stopped by to exchange greetings. He observed that I was running, which I took to mean that he noted I was in pretty good physical shape. So I answered that I was more of a swimmer than a runner.

And then he corrected himself: he meant, of course, running for Parliament.

My neighbour is a well-known journalism professor, columnist, and writer. I long ago concluded from the signs sported on his lawn during municipal, provincial, and federal elections that he or someone else in his family was staunchly Liberal. He nonetheless observed that national politics needed people like me to run. I was pleased to hear that.

My neighbour asked me if this was costing me a lot of money. My answer was "no."

Upon reflection, however, I realized that a "no" from me was not an honest reply. I was pandering to the myth that running for public office is a level playing field for anyone and everyone who might be interested. I was allowing my neighbour, familiar as he was with politics in Canada, to continue believing in a fable about the political process.

For starters, by then I had already learned that being a candidate was a full-time job. At that point I had been at it for six months. My last consulting contract had concluded over half a year earlier. The opportunity cost, measured against what I could have continued to earn if I had remained active as a senior consultant, was in the order of $10,000 per month. At that point my true cost had already amounted to more than $60,000. It would grow to over $200,000.

This is too much for most Canadians to bear.

When Carol Latimer first showed me the books of the Ottawa–Vanier Electoral District Association, I was shocked. There was nothing in the bank account. The election campaign of my predecessor Patrick Glémaud had been funded primarily by way of loans from rich EDAs in Calgary and Edmonton. Our association still owed $20,000 to one of those two associations.

The first EDA board meeting I attended was in the party room of the apartment building where Carol lived with her husband,

Will, and a couple of contented cats. I counted thirty-two people in the room. We sat in a semicircle facing the long table at which the executive of the board was bookended by a large urn of coffee on the one end and plates of cheese, crackers, and grapes on the other. The cats looked hungrily at the cheese but lacked the energy to pounce. A very large man of my age sat close beside me, leaned over, and, while gesturing toward Carol, observed, "I don't like her."

I was asked by the treasurer of the association what I was going to do about the EDA's financial situation.

I, of course, had no "rich" sponsors. I knew no one currently sitting with the CPC in the House of Commons. I had never had to raise money before, except to support sports teams by selling chocolate bars when I was in high school. The looks exchanged among board members when I said these things implied that they might need to get me replaced sooner rather than later. I learned that my candidacy had been appealing because I lived in what is statistically the wealthiest corner of the city. I was presumed to have deep pockets. When I had been asked "What are you prepared to contribute to your own campaign?" my answer should have been "Whatever it takes."

In the course of that very first meeting I set my mind to doing what I could about the financial situation of the EDA, not because I had come quickly to the conclusion that this was my job rather than that of the association, but because I could already see that no one else was going to do it. There were legal and practical limits to what I would be able to pay out of my own bank account.

This meeting presented the first of the many tests of financial commitment that would be coming my way.

I made my first commitment of family members when I told Marie that she had little choice in the matter: we were headed off on a political journey whether she liked it or not. My second commitment of family was my brother. Figuratively on bended knee, I beseeched him to help me get through the nomination convention and then, if I won the nomination, to help set the stage for an eventual campaign. By the time the writ eventually dropped, my brother would be in Jamaica, but over a period of eight months his role as intended finance officer (called the official agent) on a fledgling campaign team was emotionally reassuring.

My brother's participation proved to be much less reassuring in other respects. He minced no words. He would observe that most of the EDA members he met over the coming months were weak. He would be dismissive about much of the campaign material I was pulling together. He was impatient with the cooperative approach I was taking with the central HQ of the Conservative Party. He would exhort me to raise the money needed for a fully funded campaign (over $80,000), and he would insist that my EDA commit itself to a transfer of no less than $35K when the writ dropped. But he would not raise a finger to achieve either goal himself.

My brother had been regional director general with Public Works and Government Services Canada in the Maritimes and was then working as a consultant on various government projects. His habit had long been one of delegation, even to me as his younger brother when we were children. That the EDA had no volunteers willing to act on the various instructions he would send my way did not seem to make a difference. In effect, he wanted me to do all those things that he believed needed to be done myself. But I could not have gotten started without him.

We had always had an amicable relationship, with the utmost respect for each other's professional capabilities. I trusted his expertise and judgment and felt grateful to count him alongside Marie in my "volunteer" staff of two. I suspected from the outset, however, that my time together with my brother might not take us all the way to the finish line. I always hoped it would. But when he stepped away and out of the country only six months before the writ would drop, I was ready.

In addition to my wife and brother, I then called upon my daughters, especially Amy and Miriam, my son Gerrit, and their partners and friends. With the attendance of those close family members at the first round of my campaign team meetings, I was able to build up the numbers and — even more important — lower the median age of attendees. Had my other daughter and son, Robin and Kees, lived in Ottawa, I would have drawn them in as well.

The commitment of family went beyond their mere presence at campaign team meetings and fundraising events organized by the EDA or by Marie and me. I asked Miriam's partner, Jason, for example, to focus upon volunteer outreach and Internet communications. He proved extremely good at this, especially considering he didn't own a computer. I bought a new machine for Marie and gave him our older but fully functioning one. (Purchasing a computer for one's online communications specialist is another of the many costs that would have been impossible for me to anticipate from the outset.)

Miriam and Jason, for most of my time as a candidate, formed a happy team who together took advantage of their new computer to design and upload a number of YouTube features which, to my mind, matched the quality of what any professional could have done. They are both trained in theatre and the arts, so I should not have been surprised. What did immensely surprise me, just weeks before the election was called, was that Jason and Miriam broke up and went their separate ways. Two years later they would link up again and be married at the Naval Officers' Mess in Ottawa.

Amy helped me develop a Facebook page, which proved to be very useful as a landing spot for potential supporters surfing the web and as a repository for the pieces of my writing that didn't make it to press anywhere else. Her advice on the content of articles and intended speeches was carefully apolitical, as required by her job in Canada's public service, but always greatly appreciated. She too would part company with me and the campaign before election day.

Gerrit became a dependable go-to guy for the legwork I would need to do when campaign material required pictures and photo processing for inclusion in brochures. The amounts I paid him for those services helped him to deal with the cost of being a student at the University of Ottawa.

My commitment of family would lose me, during my nineteen months as a candidate, my brother, two of my three daughters, the relationship between Miriam and Jason, and cost me many painful rounds with Marie. I would run up against the disinclination of Marie's extended family to acknowledge what was consuming me, every minute of every day, because of their attitude toward the political party I was standing for. Among friends of many decades, a few would end all communication with me at one point or another during the period, again because of the disfavour with which they viewed the CPC.

The staying power of people I would meet and befriend within the ranks of the EDA would also be sorely tested. By the time the writ dropped, only one person of the dozens I met during the opening rounds, at the first EDA board meeting and subsequently, would still be around. You have already seen how the test of values lost me the support of Guy and Gene.

Upon my stepping into their ranks as candidate, the membership of the EDA included a half-dozen executive members, Carol, Eleanor Brady, Ross Carrothers, Guy, and Gene among them. Board members with specific functions included Gordon Peters (campaign advisor), Mark Rogal and Heather Parks (communications), Bruce Waverley (policy advisor), and Wendy (high-rise access coordinator). Only Eleanor would still be standing with me in the last five crucial weeks and on the day of the vote.

Let's now take a closer look at the people, structures, and normal operations of this creature called an electoral district association. I had expected, as recounted in my fable, that the EDA would carry me along — right to the finish line. The loss of so many volunteers who at some point had wanted to be part of their candidate's run for public office reflects both upon me as a novice candidate and upon how well EDAs are equipped to do their jobs. It says a lot about the commitment of EDA members as well.

As legally enabled organizations, electoral district associations are supposed to support Canada's recognized political parties by maintaining and building their base of supporters between elections. The EDAs are entitled to receive and spend contributions provided by citizens who want to support the political process financially.

The EDAs are therefore registered with oversight bodies, such as Elections Canada at the federal level. They must annually submit their financial statements to the federal or provincial government (depends on the political level at which they operate). In short, they must conduct themselves in an honest and transparent way as befits all organizations and associations in Canada which pay their way with public funds. The money received and expended by EDAs are public funds because of how Canada's income tax regime works. At the federal level, for example, in return for a contribution to a political party listed by the Canada Revenue Agency as an eligible recipient, the contributor receives a 75% tax credit on the amount paid.

The structure of an EDA, therefore, must include a president and a treasurer. Between them these two account for the performance and the funding of the EDA for which they, on a voluntary basis, have assumed responsibility. EDAs also typically have one or more vice-presidents, a secretary, an officer responsible for fundraising, another person focused upon membership, and so on. These are the executive members. They are chosen by a vote among board members after the annual general meeting at which the board members themselves have been chosen (often self-selected) and voted upon by all the ordinary members who attend the annual meeting.

During the period between elections, the EDAs are mandated to champion the policies of their respective political parties; to reach out to voters in the riding and solicit new members; and to convene meetings among residents where information sharing, having fun, and fundraising are the objectives. In the shorthand of electoral politics, the slogan for the work of EDAs between elections has become "Promote the Brand." For the political party which happens to be in power in Ottawa or in the capital city of a province, it is important to note that their EDAs are not agents of the government. Not that it would make any difference in the Canada of today — most EDAs are much too weak to make much of a difference.

In the case of the Conservative Party of Canada, there is an aspect of the fundraising activity that is noteworthy, as seen in how it played out at my first campaign team meeting. If a contribution is sent to the national headquarters of the Conservative Party of Canada, the association for the riding in which the contributing citizen resides will eventually receive a 10% share. If that same citizen contributes directly to the EDA, the association keeps 100% of the amount. So it would appear that EDAs and the national offices of their parties are in competition for the extremely scarce resource of voluntary contributions. Fewer than 4% of taxpaying citizens in our democratic country are regular financial contributors to the political process. What is true for the Conservative Party at the federal level is true across the board, federally and provincially, though the percentages kept and shared will differ.

Very few of the citizens who make financial contributions understand the difference between their party at the national level and their association at the riding level. In the case of my riding, even the executive was wrong about how the contributions from residents tracked their way into party and EDA coffers. At first it astonished me to learn that the national office of our party did not make it their business to correct this misperception, and then I began to see how it was in the central party interest to leave the confusion as it was.

Electoral district associations raise money not just to cover activities meant to maintain and reward the spirit of their own volunteers (bowling, pizza nights, dances). They also try to build and maintain a net balance which can be transferred to their candidate after an election is called. Or they are supposed to. The candidate would then have something to work with at the start of his or her campaign. The amount a candidate for public office is allowed to spend during an election is determined in large part by the number of voters. When the writ dropped, we candidates in Ottawa–Vanier were told we would be allowed to spend $87,000. In my case, the transferred amount in value (signs) and cash would be in the order of $30,000.

On the evening of our first campaign team meeting, Guy DesRoches, who was by then my interim team leader, was the meeting's chair. I was not optimistic.

The meeting got interesting right from the outset when Colin McSweeny, from the national office, showed up. I had not expected this. Indeed, just the day before I had advised Guy that one of our objectives must be to distance ourselves from the national office.

Colin sat opposite me. I detected in his demeanour some negative vibes in my direction, and I reacted to a comment or two by whispering to Marie, sitting beside me — "Don't let me lose control!" Frankly, to see that fellow sitting opposite me, slovenly dressed but looking so competent in his own eye, and knowing that he had not deigned it in his interest to return any of my phone calls or emails since the one time we spoke after I was acclaimed as candidate, placed me in a very negative frame of mind.

The meeting unfolded at a low key. For the longest time no one seemed motivated to contribute anything but the few platitudes that were shared about electioneering. There was a lot of silence. The fun began when Ross reacted to advice from Colin about how to prepare for a campaign financially. The target amount of $87,000 appeared well beyond the reach of an association with almost nothing in its bank account. Ross, quite calmly at first, observed, "You guys in the national office talk a good line, but you never have anything tangible to offer."

Remember, when a riding's residents contribute to the national office of the CPC, the riding receives 10% of the amount contributed; when those same residents contribute directly to the riding association, the association retains 100%. So the challenge for riding associations was to get CPC supporters to "think nationally but contribute locally."

The debate between Ross and Colin grew very tense, very quickly. Within a minute or two they were shouting at each other. Ross was elaborating upon how much Ottawa–Vanier residents contribute at the national level; Colin was stridently saying that educating residents to contribute locally rather than nationally was the EDA's job. Each was telling the other that a poor job was being done.

An interesting turn came when Colin stood to gather his stuff and walk out. His words at that point, addressed to Ross as representative of the association, were clear: "You guys are a bunch of screw-ups and you cannot expect National to save your asses." If he had actually left (which is what I was hoping he would do), that parting shot would have stayed behind, ringing in our ears. Our future relationship with the national office would have become very interesting indeed.

Instead, after an intervention by Guy, Colin slowly returned to his seat... and Ross stood up. Ross had totally lost control over his temper at this point. With his tongue darting in and out of his mouth, he shouted that the national office had zero interest in our riding and had long since satisfied itself that we were a bunch of losers. Ross lamented that, after some seven years of his working for the party, national had never taken the time to thank him for his efforts. He grabbed his stuff, and then Ross, the finance officer for the Ottawa–Vanier Conservative Association, left the building. He did not come back.

This gave Colin the opportunity to recover his cool. Ross's departure appeared to confirm Colin's negative assessment about our association's competence. Many around the table found themselves bowing toward Colin for being the more savvy, cool, calm, and collected guy.

The air actually cleared a little. One after another, those present who were also members of the association declared their confidence that the association could certainly do better than it has done in the past. The collective refrain was "We can do what National expects. We can raise the money we need. We will follow the advice National provides. We have been but minions who, quite rightly, are viewed by National to have become inconsequential in the scheme of things." I and my campaign team members said nothing.

My major challenge in the early months was to watch and learn whom in party headquarters and whom in the association I should listen to. Every piece of advice I received from one person in the association was almost certain at some point, within only hours or days, to be contradicted by another. I learned that anyone contributing to my adventure might at any time quit the association or be shoved aside by the president or the CPC. I would typically be the last to know. To commit myself too closely to anyone in particular was not a good idea.

I learned, for example, that the style of the communications team leader, Mark Rogal — entirely pleasant from my point of view — was viewed by others to be brusque and unacceptable. Guy and Carol were particularly incensed by what they viewed as his presumptive and impolite manner. When Mark produced a "doorknocker" brochure for me, with the advice that I should hit the ground running, first Carol and then others rejected its contents. By my first Christmas as a candidate, three months in, I would not yet have any material or any introductions within the Ottawa–Vanier community… except for a coffee party held in Carol's apartment building. She happened to live in the apartment building where my parents had lived for a few years before moving to a seniors' residence close to my sister's place in Quebec's Eastern Townships. The most pleasant and welcoming attendees at Carol's party had been friends of my parents. They came to the event, advertised by Carol in the foyer of the building, because they recognized my name.

The example of Mark's preparation of that introductory doorknocker is worth elaborating upon. Shortly after I was confirmed as the CPC candidate, Mark correctly decided that a one-page information piece should be prepared, one that I could use when visiting voters in the riding. He asked me for draft content about myself, and he arranged for final text to be written and translation to be done. He asked Heather, the other person on the communications team, to help him with this.

About two weeks after the photo shoot, Mark shared with me a sample doorknocker and I was asked to approve it. I did not greatly like the image Mark and Heather had selected among the many dozens of pictures taken (it looked more like a police mug shot than a political profile), but I was happy to trust their judgment about this. The text on my background was good.

The doorknocker now approved by me, Mark contacted a printer he had used for other purposes in his professional life, and about five hundred copies of the doorknocker were produced. I was ready to go!

But no. While the draft doorknocker had been shared all along the way with the executive, and while the form and content had been reviewed by the community outreach lead for our association (Gene), Carol suddenly had a fit about the thing. She exercised her executive power to issue a cease-and-desist instruction.

The doorknocker, now being printed, would not be approved by the association for use.

She advised that she would be pulling together an alternative one-pager, and that I should not start reaching out to riding residents — not even to registered CPC members — until her replacement doorknocker was in our hands.

The upset and hassle this caused among board members is best left to the imagination. Ross, for one, was extremely upset. As treasurer and finance officer, he did not want to pay for a few hundred brochures that would not be used.

In the end I footed the bill for the production of Mark's doorknocker myself, and I never asked the association executive to approve my use of them. I did use them (another national office rule broken), but only when I snuck out of the house and skulked around neighbourhoods entirely on my own initiative. I was in no position to call upon people listed as association volunteers. Carol's intervention, meanwhile, had delayed my formal introductions in Ottawa–Vanier by at least two more months. These kinds of miscommunications and inefficiencies were near daily occurrences. Every piece of printed material was a battle; every event was a massive undertaking.

There are many ways to raise money. I have already mentioned the two primary ones: selling memberships and hosting events. The third way is a little different and does not come into play until months after an election is over. This third money stream doesn't flow from voters directly: it is the government subsidy program that reimburses 60% of allowable expenses incurred campaigning.

One morning over coffee with Marie, some twelve months in, I took a close look at the accumulating numbers. When the morning's basic chores and my exercises were done, I retrieved the association's financial statement from January and compared it to the one from April the year before. The numbers did not add up at all.

I sent a long email to Guy DesRoches, observing the problems. In short, within a number of expenditure categories, there were numbers which no one had seen before and for which there were no breakdowns. Also, there were expenditures we all knew about but which had not been recorded as paid or owing. Finally, three computers which Gene said had been purchased seemed to have disappeared. The one I had made available to Jason had belonged to Marie and me.

I concluded the email by observing that we appeared to have had revenue in the order of $15,000 between January and April (thanks largely to my efforts), yet the numbers in the financial statement showed that we had gone down $2,000 in our bank account. Somewhere in the muddle there should have been $17,000 in expenses.

I did not hear back from Guy. From my brother Gerald, though, I received a pretty strident cry of alarm. One of the categories, within which undocumented expenses totalled some $8,000, was labelled "campaign expenses," but there was yet no campaign to speak of. In fact, there were *three* categories which lined themselves up with the campaign and a forecast of $27,000 in campaign expenses for the association by the end of the year, but no election had been called. Gerald advised that those costs needed to be captured differently. And I couldn't agree more.

I brought this matter to Ross's attention in an email (no reply) and forwarded the additional concern raised by Gerald to Guy and Gene (no reply). I also called the national office (no reply).

I wondered if EDAs might be allocating dollars against campaign costs so that they could get those costs repaid to the association by campaign teams after an election. If an association were in a position to say that $27,000 and more were spent by the EDA for material used by the candidate during the election, then the money could be included in the 60% that Elections Canada repays to candidates who attract at least 10% of the vote.

I worried that local associations and the national office may have developed an accounting approach that had Elections Canada contributing to the electoral district associations' ongoing pre-writ operating costs every time there was a federal election.

I eventually heard back via my brother that we were troubling ourselves about a displaying of figures that had become conventional and approved accounting. After this inspection of the books, however, I took greater care to ensure that I would not be used by my association or the national office as a conduit for public funds to flow into the association bank account immediately after the next federal election (when the subsidy is paid). I pressed for a new funding category in the EDA books. I asked that a contingencies account be set up, not labelled a campaign account, which would be closed down and the money transferred to my campaign at the time of an election. The EDA executive observed that this is what had been intended all along, and peace was restored among us. We continued onward.

By now my commitment of personal time and effort had grown to include full-time participation in the planning and delivery of both small and large scale money-raising and "brand-promoting" events. We had difficulties and tension from time to time, such as the rock-and-roll dance we were poised to feature in the first week after much of Haiti was destroyed in an earthquake, but we were always able to adjust or change tack to maintain our gathering momentum. We began to make a little money.

Thanks to the generous support of Anne Douglas, for example, we had a fantastically successful event in September 2010. That fall, as always, an election was in the air and it was time to push hard. The push began with a letter that I sent to all past and potential major donors in the riding. I drew their names from a study I had done of contributions over the past five years to the CPC at both national and local levels. To my great appreciation,

Anne had volunteered both to call all the people on the list whom I did not already know personally and to host the fundraising event. The initial idea was to have the event at her private club. By the time it happened, the event was hosted at her home. This is the letter that went out:

LETTER TO SUPPORTERS

My purpose with this letter and the accompanying material is to add to whatever you may already have heard about my candidacy. If you have not heard or read about me before, this material will bring you up to date. My goal is to build a base of committed supporters within my own neighborhood.

One of my Rockcliffe supporters will be hosting a cocktail party in the fall of this year. At that event I will say more about who I am, I will elaborate upon the reasons why I think the Ottawa–Vanier riding can be won for the Conservative Party in the next federal election, and I look forward to questions and answers being exchanged among us that will help me prepare for open-forum discussions.

This letter is my invitation to you, to consider joining me and other Rockcliffe members for the event.

Success in the political process requires money. The Ottawa–Vanier Conservative Association has begun canvassing in polls across the riding, for example, which is preceded by a distribution of literature and is accomplished by ferrying a team of volunteers through the streets. Each round of canvassing typically costs the Association about $600 in mailing fees alone.

So my invitation to have you join us for a cocktail comes with a hitch: you will be added to the list of supporters to whom I will turn not only for advice and input but for donations as well!

My wife and I are already committed to each make the maximum contribution allowable under the rules of Elections Canada. A payment to the national office of the Conservative Party is unfortunately "lost" to us at the local level because the Party only pays 10% of donations made nationally to local organizations. A payment made to the Ottawa–Vanier Conservative Association stays 100% with our Association and in support of my efforts. As we like to say within the Association: "Think nationally, but donate locally!"

Like you, my wife and I moved to Rockcliffe because we love our house and the area… and we value our privacy.

I will follow up with you, therefore, only if I learn from you that you are interested in joining us this fall (date to be decided later). Let me know if you are interested by sending me an email reply.

For more information about me I invite you to check the website www.votewestland.ca and the Facebook link at that site. There is also a link which confirms the address of the Ottawa–Vanier Conservative Association for contributions you may be able to make even before we meet in the fall.

A total of sixty-five people attended, and my presentation was well received. I began by acknowledging how important it was for a candidate to know who his or her supporters were. By this time I had already lived through the impact of negative feedback from some family members and erstwhile friends. My primary purpose now was, I said, to say "thank you" for agreeing to attend this event and for being a part of the political process in our riding.

I then spoke briefly about why I was running, and I used the opportunity to share highlights of the approach I and my campaign team were expecting to adopt. Since obtaining the funds needed for our approach to be implemented was one of my imperatives, and given the nature of my audience, I presented my plan for the campaign in the form of a pitch to investors.

"A certain return on your investment," I said, "will be a hard-fought effort." But, more than that, I dared to say that a possible return included victory for our conservative orientation to politics in a riding that had been Liberal from the get-go. "It bothers me," I said, "as a student of politics and as a competitive person, that the incumbent MP presumes the Ottawa–Vanier seat is his by divine right."

I then looked around the room and named those who had been Conservative candidates in this riding prior to me. While only one of those named was in attendance, I had this to say about Liberal Party's presumption: "Stephen Woollcombe did not believe this to be true, Kevin Friday did not believe it, Paul Benoit did not believe it, Patrick Glémaud did not believe it.

They have each run for the Conservatives in previous elections. I do not believe the Liberal presumption should be allowed to stand either."

At this point in the presentation I referred to a flip chart I had brought with me that took me through the stages of what I described as typical of military campaign planning.

"Our campaign," I said, "will focus at the tactical level, leaving strategy to the national office." At the tactical level, the "centre of gravity" of our main opponent would be his lack of results (especially on three key issues) and the fact that he had been in his spot for a very long time. My campaign would be aimed at the themes of *Too Long* and *No Results*. I concluded by re-emphasizing that those present could consider their donations to my campaign as an investment, and that the return on their investment could well be our victory in the next federal election.

You can hear in my words to those assembled that my commitment of all that it would take to win the next election had become almost total. To some extent, one might even say that I was in the process of committing my common sense: the riding had been Liberal since its creation, and no Conservative candidate in recent memory had ever reached the still-losing target of 30% of votes cast.

I left the event with a pretty good sense that most of those attending would contribute at least $400 apiece when an election was called. And they did. Their support would account for most of the $9K I would be able to raise in the first few days after the writ dropped. The timing would prove to be crucial.

Success also began coming to the EDA. When the association's bank account had grown to $38K, the national office advised us that we had moved into the top tier of electoral district associations across the country. There had been a very significant change in our fortunes from the day I had set privacy concerns aside and had become actively engaged in fund raising. The new executive of the EDA, Brock Stephens and Shaun Warren having replaced Carol and Ross at an annual general meeting of the association in March 2010, were in a position to assure me that the EDA would cover the cost of lawn signs for the next election ($8K), the cost of printing and distributing material that I had already developed and tabled before them (another $3K), and more.

Brock was confident that the association would transfer at least $19K in cash to the campaign team when the writ was dropped. When one took into account the cost of the signs and initial rounds of printing, the total value would be very close to what had been targeted six months earlier when my brother had first grumbled his way into the business.

For me, foregone revenues (contract income no longer possible) were by then in the order of $190,000. To maintain our lifestyle, I had to close down my RRSP ($37,000). One of my informal purchases was $500 spent on that ski jacket I mentioned earlier. Marie will no longer let me wear it in her company. This jacket features the CPC logo on each shoulder and on the front left pocket, and the words "Team Westland" standing proudly tall and centred on the back. While the notion was that a great many "Team Westland" jackets would become visible on the streets of our riding, mine was the only one ever purchased. It now hangs permanently in the closet at the cottage.

CHAPTER 5.

THE TEST OF LEADERSHIP

Novice candidates as described in this book are not junior in their background. We are Canadian citizens and residents in our ridings who have built solid careers while keeping our eyes on politics and political issues. Because of our commitment to family, we have been involved in neighbourhood and school activities since our kids were little. In the wide range of our contributions to our communities and to the workplace, we have become direction-setters among friends and neighbours and leaders in our professional endeavours.

Political parties are not looking for leadership from their candidates. Political commentators have long been making the point that political parties, not just the CPC, are looking for representatives who will carry a few centrally conceived slogans into the public forum. They are looking for candidates who will toe the line.

Their great worry is that "rogue" candidates will slip past EDA and central HQ selection committees. Rogue candidates are the ones who speak their own minds or, even worse, contradict the content of messages that are meant to be exactly the same across the country (for a federal election) or province. Pundits and columnists love rogue candidates. The longer a candidate has been out there meeting the people, the greater the risk that the candidate will go rogue.

That is one of the main reasons, it appears to me, why political parties often begin their drives to find and appoint candidates only a few months before an election is expected. The culture of elections has become a crunch culture. Everyone comes together — the candidate and his or her team — with sometimes only weeks or even days remaining before the writ drops.

The novice candidate has only one choice if appointed at the last minute: do what you are told. Follow your instructions to the letter. The campaign literature a candidate is copied on when the election is imminent has a clear, if underlying, message: a candidate who manages his or her own campaign is a fool. Even the candidate's significant other is at best an irritant.

The trouble is that novice candidates are most definitely not fools. We are people who have become successful at managing large and small enterprises and at managing what happens in our own personal lives. The novice who steps into electoral politics while there is still time to make sense of what is happening will apply his or her skills and do whatever is possible to help shape the outcome.

In the test of privacy, you had to reveal your intentions to your personal and professional networks. Then you met face to face with riding residents, boldly telling them all about your values even though your association was convinced that your individuality didn't matter and that this election was all about data. You have committed money, family, friends, time, and considerable effort. You came through it... you think. And here you are still standing. You have come this far, and you now want to be sure that your future is in good hands.

This takes us back for another look at the electoral district association, because the novice, being new to the electoral process, has learned in his or her career to look for leadership from those who are most experienced.

One thing the EDA did on its own was initiate a proposal for your candidacy to party headquarters. Within days of your name going into the hat, and after you have obtained confirmation from your local police that you do not have a record of concern to law enforcement agencies, the folks in headquarters will have done whatever research they do when strangers' names are forwarded to their office. But they will be in no rush to transmit a final approval. They don't have to confirm you as the official party candidate until a full forty-eight hours after the writ drops. So even if you win at a nomination convention, you will be a candidate-in-waiting. You will not have certainty. This is important. It means that if you begin to exert leadership too soon, by stepping out in front of your EDA and becoming rogue, you can be dropped like a hot potato with only a moment's notice.

Exerting leadership would nonetheless become an imperative much sooner than I had expected.

To stand for nomination, a potential candidate needs the endorsement of twenty-five party members, and you must get these on your own. This sets novices like you and I immediately back upon our heels. Being a novice means you are highly unlikely to know who among your friends and neighbours belong to the party. Your EDA contacts must have suspected that this would be the case when they asked you — a stranger to them all — to step up to the plate. But you followed through. You had to do this on your own. The first baby steps toward your assumption of a leadership role have been taken.

The next step must be taken as you prepare for the nomination convention. In order to become a candidate, you have to make a payment of at least $1000 to party headquarters, and you need to have a legally designated finance officer handle this. Your EDA will not take this on because there may a number of candidates vying for the nomination. In the previous chapter, you saw how this payment was only the beginning of many more. You saw that I turned to my brother for help. On both fronts — the first of many draws upon your personal bank account and the tentative reaching out for a supporting team — you will find that your need and urge to take charge will grow.

Although an election may not be called for many months, you

will feel that it is time to get going — *now*. Your EDA may not care to get ready so soon and may not agree. Your EDA and your party will want you to stay low-key. A lot will be said about building "name recognition" and about elections being won or lost between the periods of the writ, but your direction, as I have said, will instead be to build up data on the voting intentions of riding residents. At the doors, you will be discouraged from sharing your values and discussing the issues: you are supposed to ask "Which party will you be voting for in the next election?"

You will find that sitting idle and doing nothing — if that is the only alternative to collecting data — is unacceptable. You would rather get going entirely on your own if that is what it takes. The obstacle that sits between an impossible science and an out-of-vogue human experience is *you*. You will have to decide for yourself which way to turn.

If you decide to go for the human experience, as I did, you will need help. This is where the commitment of family and friends begins to count. You will have to beg their indulgence as you begin to also beg for their money and their time and their effort. Those who agree to join you will all be first-timers too, of course. They will not know how to proceed.

This means you will have to read all the material your association has given to you; you will have to teach the friends and family members who have agreed to join you; and, for a while, you will have to lead and manage them. If the party you will be representing is one that your family and friends do not personally like, your challenge will be a little greater.

Waiting for your EDA to take charge is not an option. Its members will not have the energy to take on the tasks and work you want to have done in the way that you want to do it. Additionally, though you may have thought you were approached because you seemed uniquely qualified, you will learn that your EDA approached a number of other potential candidates as well — all of them politicos. Electoral district associations across the country see candidate nomination conventions as an opportunity to bring in new energy, new members, and new money. EDAs do not expect to be very busy between elections in discussions on policy, either within the ranks or — most definitely not — with the public at large.

In my fable, electoral district associations appeared to be the solid base upon which participatory democracy operates. But one of your first mistakes was to assume that the EDA members who helped to usher you away from your private life would do everything possible to support you. As a novice candidate, your expectation is that the board members and executive of your EDA will always be there to hold your hand, teach you when teaching is necessary, and backstop you with the talent and the financing you need. This will not be so.

It would be nice if, when an election is called, EDA members would become the ones who constitute your campaign team and, if you lose the upcoming election, welcome you back into the ranks of the EDA as a contributing member of the party. You would then have the lifelong association with politics that you had so often thought about when you were out there making a good living. But EDAs are not strong at all, and that is really too bad.

In my fable, democracy in this country was imagined to be a space filled on a daily basis with discussion of political issues within families, among friends and neighbours, and within places of work, not a phenomenon that finds its expression only in the "one person, one vote" activity of election day. After all, legislation concerning the individual and collective rights of us all surely matters. Policies on how our country relates to other countries around the globe on trade issues, security issues, and social issues matter as well. Programs launched and funded to respond to the needs of Aboriginal people are important. Programs that deal with the care of children and of older citizens are important. A successful democracy would thrive on continual engagement with our neighbours on these issues and others.

Whereas the novice candidate expects his or her riding association to provide the comfort and strength a neophyte requires, ordinary members will be looking to the candidate to bring comfort and strength to their unhappy ranks. All their different interests have likely not been managed very well by the association's executive. Ordinary members will look to you as their new leader.

The board, and especially the executive, of your association, however, will welcome you with a wary eye. They will not want the new guy or gal on the block to upset their own political or personal agendas. They took on the added burden of board responsibilities and executive office, after all, in order to advance those agendas. They know that novice candidates are just passing through. After the next election, which the novice almost always loses, it will be back to business as usual.

You will find that even if the number of your EDA's active members has dwindled down to a paltry dozen, the association is riveted by internecine struggles. Each and every board member will have a different reason for being there. The members of the executive will greatly value their exposure to sitting members of Parliament and of legislative assemblies, perhaps even to ministers. They will not want you to get in the way. The EDA's ordinary members have been chafing under the desultory directions coming from their board and executive for a long time and will be counting on you to step in and throw the bums out.

It will surprise you (but you will get used to it) that the members of your EDA executive and board are much less interested in your success as a fledgling politician than you had believed would be the case. Their future, you see, is not dependent upon *your* future. You are a novice candidate for a reason. The odds are that your party has not been much of a contender in your riding for quite some time. If being a candidate in your riding provided a reasonable chance to get elected, you would have been bowled over in the nomination process by politicos who judged their opportunity to be a competitive one. Politicos are always hovering about. Novice candidates come and go.

If you want to stay in the game, you must find a way to endure the test of leadership. You must prepare for an election and protect your reputation even while your forbearance with regard to the EDA members' personal struggles and traumas begins to fall off to rejection and anger. You will not be able to dismiss the EDA as you might have dismissed the board of your small business. Your future as a candidate depends more upon the goodwill of your EDA than upon your own proven capabilities.

EDAs and campaign teams are different creatures from each other. They differ in their purpose, their legal status, and their focus. EDAs are there for the long term. Campaign team energies are focused on the immediate term. But campaign teams have no standing between elections. These differences are a cause for considerable confusion and tension. If you do not make the two structures work in parallel, you risk sitting exposed and unprepared on voting day.

All the way along, therefore, you will have to manage issues of overlap and transition between the EDA and campaign team structures. The latter will ultimately be the most important for you, but until an election is called, the former — the electoral district association — is the only structure that legally exists. If you are a candidate for an extended period, you will constantly have to run your shadow team with one hand and respond as best you can to the performance of your EDA executive and board members with the other. You are almost certain to feel duplicitous toward individuals and sometimes even disloyal. It is counter to your leadership training and your experience to act this way. It will not be easy.

When I reflect on my nineteen months as a candidate, I would say the trigger which set off my determination to fully control my own destiny was pulled by Gordon Peters, at a lunch in late January, four months after I had made initial contact with my party's EDA in Ottawa–Vanier.

Gordon was the fellow who had sat himself beside me at my first EDA board meeting and affirmed that he did not like Carol Latimer's leadership style. He was the one who, among all the board and executive members, had most impressed me, not only because of his large size (in both height and strength) but also because of his professional background (assistant deputy minister in the federal government). He had run a successful campaign or two in other areas of Ottawa, so his street creds were good as well.

My EDA had named Gordon as my interim campaign manager. When Carol subsequently drove him out of the association, Gordon remained with me as an advisor, and I gave myself over to his leadership on the development of an eventual campaign plan. I hoped he would stay with me and take control.

At that lunch in late January, where I believed we were going to talk about an adjusted version of his ambitious plan for a campaign, he declared: "Rem, I have had enough!" He would not be continuing.

His reasons concerned the continuing poor relations he was having with EDA members, observing (correctly, in my view) that whatever he proposed would be for naught if the association was not prepared to help him stitch the pieces together between now and the time an election was called. "We have no volunteers to fill in the walk sheets for Voter ID data; we have no money to do this by telephone calls; we have no fundraisers planned that will raise more than a few dollars above cost. Frankly, Rem, you don't have a chance." I paid for the lunch.

To say that I was put out by Gordon's withdrawal would be an understatement. I certainly could understand his pessimism, but the fact was that my work to have association members contribute their money locally was beginning to have an effect. We were out of debt, greatly helped by Carol's success in convincing one of our two loaning EDAs to forgive the debt we owed them. If no election were to be called for a few months, the association would have the money to begin doing the things Gordon wanted to see done. Gordon, however, was not persuaded. He was now off my team.

It was time for me to assume agency over what was going to happen between then and election day, but I had to do this in ways that would not give the EDA or the CPC cause to replace me with someone else.

I learned that most candidates begin building campaign teams, entirely separate from their associations, when they organize themselves for a nomination convention. Because I had been acclaimed, I had not had to do this.

I believe I gave a very serious effort to working with those members of my EDA who seemed interested in helping me along. In a brief speech at an EDA board meeting shortly after becoming my party's designated candidate for Ottawa–Vanier, I said that I hoped to draw my entire campaign team from the ranks of those who were then sitting at the executive table or elsewhere in the room. I truly meant that. In parallel, of course, I was not about to let go of the few friends and family members who had been prepared to help get me through a nomination process if that had been necessary. I had already begun building a shadow team even if I did not really know it yet.

Six months in, I counted twenty-six potential team members, about twenty of whom I viewed to be serious. I hoped I would soon have a core group to which I would be able to turn for reassurance and confidence-building regardless of what happened within the EDA.

Most of the people on my list were family or friends. Most had decidedly Liberal or NDP orientations. One of these was Colin Lindley, a friend going way back to when I was in sixth grade in Quebec City. He had recently given serious thought to running for the Greens. Only three on my list of potential campaign team members were currently CPC or association board members. None of the others had any political experience at all. While odd, this collection of characters gave me the courage — because of the mere fact that they existed at all and that they appeared to be friendly — to think things might start to get better. Perhaps the makeup of my team would lend me an appeal that went beyond my party's brand. Conservatism as branded by the CPC is not a big seller in Ottawa–Vanier. I would need at my side people who agreed that I would be the best representative for the riding in the House of Commons regardless of party affiliation.

It's a good thing I kept my options open. As the time went by, my campaign team underwent as many shifts in composition as did the EDA. In fact, by the time the election would be called, all but one of those assembled at my initial campaign team meeting would have parted company.

A late addition to the team, one who joined only months before the writ dropped and had to quit within days after the election period began, asked innocently, "What is it about you, Rem, that explains all those people leaving?" It was a good question!

Upon reflection, I allowed that I had an evolving, but always firm, idea about how I wanted to engage in an eventual campaign. I had had enough of the empty promises and lack of follow-through by EDA members who, while seeking to have influence over my candidacy, were at war with each other or even with the CPC head office. I was looking for people who could be counted upon to deliver results. For many of my initial cohort of campaign team volunteers, an electoral success by the CPC was not high on their personal agenda. I welcomed creative ideas and independent action by others, but everyone's room to manoeuvre had to be limited by the parameters of a basic plan I had begun to pull together in the days after Gordon quit. To move beyond the plan would always be okay, but I would need to see that the resources (people, money, skills) were in place before any expansion of the plan happened.

In effect, drawing from my experience as a senior manager, I was implementing a business-plan approach. The ingredients of the plan — in this case consisting of public messages, door-knocking and other campaign-style activities, money-raising events, and so on — were all being laid out and funded, with responsible people assigned to each separate component of the plan.

I told my friend that the people I invited to join the campaign team all have jobs. "For them," I said, "my demands become too time-consuming to match easily with the time they must allocate to professional pursuits. Many of the people who belong to the EDA and who also want to help me do not have jobs, and they do not have jobs for a reason. They are not the most dynamic folks. The unemployed people around me are hoping my journey might lead them toward steady jobs. I can do nothing for them while still only a candidate, and they feel it hard to invest too highly in me given my very low chances."

One of the reasons EDAs are weak is because of the people who constitute the membership. My hope is that EDA memberships across the country will grow over the years to come and will gain the wide range of competencies which reflect the capacities of individual Canadians everywhere in the country. We need novices not only to stand for public office but also to join the ranks of our EDAs. As you will see, late in the day I gave serious consideration to resigning as candidate and running for a position on the board of my EDA instead.

The problem is that most of us are busy. We are busy with our families and our jobs. We have enough to do on a daily basis. Even those with a notion that we might run for public office if the circumstances are right are unlikely to find the time to be active in the EDA that represents our party of choice in the riding where we live. The members of our riding EDAs, therefore, are mostly those who have the time. They are the unemployed or the underemployed. The few on our EDAs who have full-time jobs miss most of the association's board and executive meetings. They are too busy to make it even to evening meetings.

These days, many of those who get actively involved in the work of EDAs, furthermore, often have ulterior motives. It may not always have been this way. The few who appear successful in their work are seeking opportunity, through political connections, to do better still. Those who have experienced pain in their lives such as the loss of a loved one to avoidable accidents or violent crime want, in the case of my party, to influence politicians to get hard on crime. Those who secretly smoke marijuana in their basements want to have politicians tell the police to back off. There are also those whose views are too radical, on the left or on the right of our political spectrum, for friends and colleagues to listen very long to what they need to say. Those folks want to vent their spleens in the company of others whom they believe to be like-minded.

For the longest time, even as I began more and more to flex my own muscles, Carol Latimer stayed in the back of my mind as a campaign manager in waiting. She was usually full of fun, with a sharp wit and a sharp mind. Unfortunately, her sharpness cut in a multitude of ways. I was never able to fully trust her.

Carol's capacity to see things clearly and to think things through was impressive. But her sharp edge included a very low level of tolerance for people whose ideas did not match — in her view — the quality and relevance of her own. She was almost always right about her own ideas being the best ones, but her attitude lost her the support she needed from others. Carol was a lifesaver for me in many ways, but she had a profound fear of failure. She could see around corners, and she could see the demons waiting for her. She could think her way through to logical conclusions, but she cowered when her conclusions were challenged. She was rarely able to push to completion the production of material she had herself pulled together. Carol welcomed me with open arms, and I was extremely pleased to find someone like she waiting for me after I was acclaimed. Unfortunately for us both, I suppose, I stopped being a candidate who did only what I was told long before Carol gave up trying to make me do what she instructed. Carol was never able to shift her focus from the standard way in which EDAs and campaign managers attempt to deliver results, namely, using central party messages and ordering the candidate about.

One day we fell into a conversation about politics these days. There is still a core of legitimate politics, I said, which involves discussion, debate, and persuasion. For these purposes, one uses meaningful oral exchanges (longer than thirty seconds), letters, print media, television, the Internet, and so on. In order for a candidate to engage in this kind of politics, which require the candidate to be personally engaged, the resource that is required above all others is personal time. Around this legitimate core, however, there is a bloodsucking industry looking for money. That industry sells tools such as Voter ID, GOTV ("get out the vote" systems), DVC (direct voter contact), and so on to EDAs. "I think that this industry does not contribute to politics," I said. Whereas this industry may make a difference in close races, where getting people to the polls can move final numbers into the victory zone, its focus is upon people as digits. This, to my mind, is part of the reason political participation in all forms is going down rather than up. I had no interest in using those tools at all.

Most of the money that is required for elections these days is attached to what the bloodsuckers want. To obtain accurate data on the scale the data-gathering industries tell us *we* want (ideally on 100% of voters) requires a very large team, and money, working throughout the periods between elections. I pointed out to Carol that we in Ottawa–Vanier had a very small team (only five or six dependable members), no money, and an information base to start from that was wholly out of date — and even then on only a thousand or so of the sixty thousand residents in our riding of voting age. We had information on about 1% of voters, and it was poor information at that.

I observed that I did not need a big election team in order to do what little I thought was required for legitimate politics. I observed that much of the work of larger campaign teams would be work I had little interest in. This is why, I said, I was in no hurry to find a replacement for Gordon.

Carol got quite agitated. In her assessment I was not bloody-minded enough to win the upcoming election. I must stop getting caught up in the humanity of the exercise. I needed to make executive decisions about who is performing well and who is not. Her bottom line was that I should have fired Gordon right off the bat because he had his priorities wrong. His priority should have been money-making rather than campaign planning. I now needed to fire Guy DesRoches, the EDA member who had stepped forward to give me a hand but who had failed in his role as fundraiser. And I needed to fire Gene Pierce, whose manner and approach had offended Carol long before I came on board. The clarity of her arguments nonetheless begged the question of who would remain standing.

As an aside, it is interesting to note that Carol was not the only one who thought me not bloody minded enough to succeed in the electoral process. Colin McSweeny, the fellow in the national party office who oversaw the work of all EDAs in eastern Ontario, growled after one of his meetings with my EDA board and executive, "They've all got to go! You need a scorched-earth approach!" And soon enough, they all went.

To keep campaign preparations in hand, I created a leadership circle within which I would always be the first among equals. As volunteers stepped into and out of that circle, the only human constant was me. Another constant was the developing campaign plan.

Those who felt they could not be supportive of the plan moved on, and those who came on board were asked by me to read the plan and be sure they could play by the rules set down therein.

Everyone who stepped forward to become a part of my journey was assigned to a position, alongside which the tasks for that position were laid out. I told anyone coming to me that I wanted no volunteers on my campaign team who were also members of the EDA. My assumption of leadership was becoming total.

And thank goodness it was! At the EDA's late-April annual general meeting, attendance was three times the usual number, most of the people attending being new members signed up from among Parliament Hill political staffers who resided in Ottawa–Vanier. By the end of the meeting, not a single member of the EDA I had met shortly after being appointed candidate still sat on the board or executive.

This was when Brock Stephens, a member of the Prime Minister's Office, became the new EDA president. This was when Shaun Warren replaced Ross Carrothers as treasurer. They, and all the others, were young politicos. Whereas the average age of our EDA members before the AGM had perhaps been forty-five, it was now more like thirty. As their candidate, I stood out as a fellow twice the average age.

Marie and I could not decide whether this hijacking of a weak EDA by young politicos should be understood as a compliment to me or as a bold statement from the national office that the Ottawa–Vanier electoral district association was broken and that perhaps its candidate was suspect as well. I wondered whether my own position as designated candidate for the next federal election had become uncertain. Perhaps I would be the next to go.

We learned over time that the hijacking was simply that: a takeover by ambitious young staffers who were looking to pad their resumés. The national office had less to do with it than I initially had thought. But one thing was certain: because a new team was in place that was trusted by the national office, the national office would become much less concerned in a direct way about what was happening in Ottawa–Vanier.

I found myself being drawn to the message in the poem "Invictus," written in 1875 by William Ernest Henley. I wanted, desperately, to continue being the master of my fate. I had often felt as if my party and the EDA wanted to the captain of my soul. I wondered if the struggle would get harder in the days ahead.

My developing "basic plan" for a campaign became a touchstone that saved me from despair again and again. Because of the basic plan, I always knew where I was going. I felt I was in control, even though there would continue to be good days and bad days. An early version of the plan, displayed below, was added to collectively by my inner circle. It evolved constantly, but at any one moment in time, the plan had to be read and subscribed to by everyone who wanted to become and remain part of the venture. This evolution was not dramatic: the plan stayed largely the same, with only a few substantive adjustments, right up until the writ dropped. In particular, the rule that changes to the plan would require confirmation that the necessary resources were available was never changed.

When you read the basic plan, you will note the key role of the official agent. This is the second of only three people, in addition to the candidate, who must be in place in order for a campaign to be legal. The third person is the official auditor, whose job begins after the campaign is over and who must affirm to Revenue Canada that all the books for the campaign were in order and all revenues and expenses were legal.

The official agent is the finance officer. This is the person who receives the money and writes the cheques. This is the person who carries the greatest responsibility, apart from the candidate, for what might go wrong. This is the person who could go to jail along with the candidate if legal errors or purposeful deceit amount to even a few thousand dollars. I assured Priscilla Hammond, who became my official agent after my brother went off to Jamaica and after former EDA treasurers Ross Carrothers and Dan Gregory declined the position, that she would be fully in charge of the money.

You can see that I was looking for a bare-bones approach, one that would be easy to manage yet leave a good impression upon the CPC and the electorate in our riding. I actually found myself moving toward the highlights of what my brother Gerald had advised from the outset, but with a greater sense of fun than he had displayed. My brother had become certain that I would lose. I no longer wanted to hear that from anyone. My approach included marketing simple messages in doorknocker-style material, and counted upon volunteers for the sole purpose of delivering the material to as many doors as possible in the course of the campaign. On the side, we would play with the Internet, and, of course, I would do the meet-and-greets and the open forum debates that are still part of riding-level electioneering.

"TEAM WESTLAND" BASIC PLAN FOR THE CAMPAIGN

To be added to only if additional activities proposed are confirmed by the official agent to be fully resourced (people, money, and time)

EXPECTATIONS FROM THE ASSOCIATION

1. Signs prepared pre-writ and ready to go ($15K value to the campaign) (Gene Pierce/campaign preparations manager)
2. Cash transfer at the start of the campaign: $30K (Priscilla Hammond/official agent)

PRE-WRIT FOCUS OF THE CAMPAIGN TEAM

3. Press the association to do Voter ID, candidate recognition (events, high-rise coffees, ads) and to raise money (Guy DesRoches/interim campaign coordinator)
4. Ensure candidate can meet legal imperatives for a campaign quickly (120 names of supporting voters) (Priscilla Hammond/official agent)

CONDUCT OF THE CAMPAIGN (POST-WRIT)

5. Within the first three days, provide support to candidate and official agent to ensure the campaign is legal and ready for financing.

- No cost. Lead is with interim campaign coordinator (Guy DesRoches). This activity will also involve the Official Agent (Priscilla Hammond) and the candidate.

6. Locate office space appropriate for bare-bones campaign plan (additional space to be leased only if resources are provided) (Marie and Eleanor Brady/campaign office manager)

- Up to $6K allocated for office, plus up to $7K for outfitting and operations. Lead is with campaign manager and office manager (assisted by Priscilla, Lynda, Elias).

7. Locate signs across the riding, oversee signage throughout campaign, and add new signs (use volunteers) to greatest extent possible.

- Up to $15K in signs (see bullet #1 above). Lead is with ground operations manager (Gene and Rob Waters).

8. Do final printing of "chair" flyer and of key brochure, to be delivered by lit-drops throughout campaign (use volunteers).

- Up to $15K allocated. Lead is with volunteers coordinator or outreach manager.
- When volunteers come to the Office they are asked to help with signs and/or to help deliver "chair" flyer and brochure, and/or host candidate on a walk-about in their neighbourhoods, and/or act as scrutineers.

9. Maintain list of all public events (candidate debates, media boards, etc.), coordinate times with the candidate, and accompany/prepare candidate as required. (Eleanor Brady/campaign office manager)

- Transport, refreshments, etc. for candidate and candidate partner on the trail (Colin Lindley). Up to $500 allocated.

10. Do final preparation of prepared ads (select from three already available) and submit to print media as funds may allow.

- Up to $5K allocated. Lead is with media supervisor or outreach manager (names to be provided).

11. Do neighbourhood canvassing (meet-the-candidate) as time and volunteer support permit.

- Up to $5K allocated, for refreshments and transport support. Lead is with campaign preparations manager (Gene Pierce) or volunteers coordinator. See bullet #7 above.

12. Prepare for closing party (day of election).

- Up to $2K allocated. Lead is with volunteers coordinator or campaign preparations manager.

13. Remuneration (campaign manager, official agent, official auditor)

- $10K allocated.

The addition of any activities to this plan, if fully resourced (a firm precondition) will require prior agreement from the official agent that no items on the above list must be displaced in order to stay within the maximum expenditure allowed by Elections Canada for the campaign.

Forecasted cost of the campaign: $65,500.00

One of the ingredients in the plan that gave me special satisfaction was a one-page cardboard piece we referred to as the "chair" flyer. The idea for this had been shaped in large part by Marie. From the outset I wanted a new kind of poster. If I had stayed under the leadership of the EDA, a cookie-cutter reiteration of the standard national messaging would have resulted. As it was, we did something a little different.

The image of a broken chair appeared under the phrase "This

seat belongs to all of us!" on the top of the large postcard. "Let's fix it!" appeared on the bottom. This idea took clear aim at the presumption of Liberal ownership of the Ottawa–Vanier "seat" and the consequent collapse of the democratic principles which has resulted. The back of the postcard featured a repaired chair with "Rem Westland, Member of Parliament" festooned upon it, along with an Internet address that provided for follow-up by interested residents. It was clever, it poked fun, it was funny. It became, with a few adjustments, a thing of beauty. When the writ dropped, we printed sixty thousand copies and sent them via Canada Post to all homes in the riding at a cost that was within the budget of the bare-bones plan.

Another important component in the plan became my outreach on Facebook. It was free, and it became a great place to store not only photo and video content but also extended opinion pieces and writing on current events. In my daughter Amy, I had a savvy manager of this component. I knew that party HQ kept a close eye on both my Facebook page and my website, but still I used this page with confidence. Even before I became confirmed as the official candidate in the riding, I wrote on that page exactly what I meant to say, and only once was I ordered by party headquarters to pull something down.

Meanwhile, my daughter Miriam and her partner, Jason, helped me create four video vignettes, which we posted to YouTube, each vignette designed to address local issues. In one video, on a background of crescendoing classical music, one saw the images of the bridge, Rockcliffe, and King Edward traffic — the sitting MP's three main campaign issues in each campaign since he had first been elected — interspersed with the most cherubic face of Mauril Bélanger that I have ever seen. At the near top of the rising music, in the background, appeared the words "No Results." Then, at the top of the screen, one saw my image floating toward centre stage, looking professional and somewhat stern. The impact was laughter.

While I was giving order to my campaign team and its functions, Marie was ordering her priorities, too. She had been contemplating early retirement from her job as a counsel with the Department of Justice. She had wanted more time to help me in this venture but now decided to work one more year and stop on the day that she qualified for an unreduced pension (thirty years' service).

While I had always supported Marie's plan to leave the public service early and had given her all kinds of arguments for why this made sense, a decision to stay gainfully employed longer — with an income in the range of $150K — was certainly the most logical one. Any reasonable person could predict with almost complete certainty that there would be a federal election within the coming year. Whether I won or lost, the end of my political journey would be the more logical time for the two of us to regroup and conclude upon our way ahead.

CHAPTER 6.

THE TEST OF ENDURANCE

It takes courage to step into the electoral process. And it takes tremendous stamina to stay with it, especially if you begin long before an election is called. You will have good days and bad days, thrilling highs and depressing lows. The lows will be much more frequent than the highs. You will be tempted to quit many times.

Along the way you will be regularly reminded that your status as designated candidate could be changed any moment up to the day after the election is called. That will be one of the lows, each time someone notes it. This will remind you that you have to keep your nose clean — someone "better" really could come along between now and the election, and your role as candidate could be terminated with little notice.

Given what a surprise this turn in your life has been for just about everyone who knows you, from time to time the fragility of your situation will unhinge you. This could end with you retreating to your private life with your tail between your legs before the next election ever happens.

Unless your party has been quietly preparing all along for someone else to step into the role you are playing, however, should you get this far along the gauntlet you will probably be endorsed by the leader of your party when the writ drops. You will have proven your mettle with respect to values and commitment, and you will have kept your leadership initiatives under the radar. When that writ drops, you will become a politician without elected office, rather like being a writer without any publications.

In your private life, meanwhile, your welcome among erstwhile friends will have come to an end. They will no longer be curious about you. A few, the ones you have known for the longest time, will have held out a hope that you would come to your senses, quit your party, and laugh about the aborted venture over a beer. But that has not happened.

When you get left off the invitation list for a friendly neighbourhood event, as I was when my community organized potluck dinners at embassy homes in Rockcliffe, it won't be personal. You can safely assume that the coordinators did not want to "pollute" the event with politics. Inviting the sitting MP to the same event is another matter. Successful MPs, through their own parliamentary missives and by the inclusion of their highly partisan comments in local newspaper columns, become part of the establishment. Opponents like you and I represent debate and tension.

If you or a member of your team attend a community meeting and dare raise policy issues for discussion or debate, there will be a collective shushing. "Don't politicize this meeting": you'll hear this a lot at public gatherings during the pre-election period. In my case, I stopped going to events organized by my own community organization because of how unwelcome I had begun to feel. Chalk these experiences up as a low.

While interest in talking about politics at the local level is almost zero, the intensity of feeling about politics is nevertheless very high. When you knock on doors, when you stop by local businesses, or when you collar people in pseudo-public spaces like malls and restaurants, you will find that most people would rather you had left them alone. If you press on, you are much more likely to be told "I hate your party" or "I hate those other guys as much as you do" than to find yourself engaged in meaningful debate.

Politicos are quite happy about this. For them, rather like for some religious groups proselytizing in the streets, a limited time for self-introduction and to get the message out is good enough to stroke egos and confirm intent (to score points with their party). The negativity they encounter if they press on with a potential voter is nothing compared to the insults hurled during Question Period in the House of Commons and provincial legislative assemblies anyway.

The novice who hopes that epithets can be spun off into serious discussion is naive. Though you have been primed by your background to talk seriously about the issues, you will have to adjust to being brushed off or insulted. The candidate has no other recourse to respond to an insult than to smile and reach out to the next random passerby or resident. But each time this happens is another low.

The fact is that, along with political financing, messaging in politics has become centralized. Residents' focus is upon what is said and done in Ottawa or in the provincial capital, not in the riding. Riding candidates, once elected, mostly sit on the backbenches. People who are running for election are simply party representatives who hope to replace whichever local-riding person has been keeping the bench warm.

Electoral district associations have become like franchise operations. Political party headquarters can be compared to the central offices of operations like Harvey's and McDonald's. Franchisees are expected to set themselves up in accordance with the dictates from the centre. Electoral district association messaging is akin to the making of hamburgers and hot dogs: each and every time the same, fried or broiled according to formulas issued by the boss.

Programs based upon the so-called science of politics reinforce the message that persuasion, customized to the needs and understanding of community members, is no longer on the menu. Indeed, just as Harvey's and McDonald's have built up their own client base over the years, the EDAs of political parties believe they know who their customers are. Candidates are told not to waste time soliciting votes from another party's client base. "Go for the low-hanging fruit," get your own people out to vote, and hope that the others stay home.

In this environment, getting ready for an eventual election can be a discouraging business for the novice. And the longer the novice is in business before the sprint toward an election begins — when the writ is dropped — the greater the discouragement.

Between elections, EDAs can reach out to the public to raise money, increase their memberships, and promote their party's brand. The candidate designated by the EDA and its party to run in the next election can be used to help achieve those goals. The candidate cannot, however, actively campaign for election. Active campaigning for amateurs like you can only happen, and money for that express purpose can only be raised and spent, during the election itself. The sitting MP, however — the only professional politician in the competition — has all the resources and opportunities available to make re-election fairly easy.

For the novice candidate who wants to devote a lot of his or her time to the electoral process during the pre-writ period, this limitation appears unfair. While you are knocking on the doors of residents who are manifestly disinclined to engage in politics ("I didn't know there was an election going on?"), the elected representative for your riding can do whatever it takes to retain his or her seat. You will find that sitting members get more and more active with their newsletters and public appearances as the rumoured date of an election gets closer and closer. You will find yourself nipping at the little things and endlessly planning something better while the person you want to replace is out there securing his or her place on the bench simply by leveraging the role of an incumbent. It is legitimate… but to you, the novice candidate, it will seem unfair.

You will chafe every time you are told by your EDA handlers and by the politicos in your party's central office, "Just relax. Just do as we say." Sometimes you will feel very strongly that simply going along with them would be so much easier. But, damn it, your background has you primed to function very differently. In an age where image and distance are safer bets than substance and personal contact, you, unfortunately, won't be able to help yourself. You will always feel the imperative of going "old-style," which is to say delivering "direct voter contact" in a truly meaningful way.

I believe that all novice candidates, if on the election trail for longer than the short period of the writ, will want to behave as I did. This is likely another reason why novice candidates will become more rare in the years to come. Young and aspiring careerists, however, submit themselves readily and even enthusiastically to the directions from on high. They'll run through the gauntlet at a good clip. They have nothing to lose. By being so willingly malleable in the hands of party and EDA executive members, politicos earn the trust of their political establishment. If elected to the House of Commons, they confirm, they will be team players for the political party of their choice.

Novices who remain true to their principles send a message to the party that they will continue to stand on their own records of achievement. Closer to the end of the run, the message to party insiders will be that a candidate is becoming "difficult to manage." Those words were attached to my candidacy right up to the end, written on a piece of paper that my campaign coordinator had left on his desk when my official agent cleaned up our office the day after the vote.

In September of the year before the election, I was invited to attend a barbeque in Edwards, Ontario. The guest of honour was Prime Minister Stephen Harper. As these things go, the barbeque was a special event for me. This event was one of the highs that helped me endure the long run of lows.

First, I was pleased to be taken to the prime minister's private suite (overlooking a crowd of about nine hundred people) and hosted there until the PM arrived. He had been briefed well enough to know my name. His wife, Laureen, whom I had met at a fundraiser earlier in the year, was pleased to confirm my identity. We shook hands, exchanged a few words, and had some pictures taken.

When folks ask "What was the prime minister's approach with you?" my answer is that I had a sense of commiseration. His first words to me were "It's not easy doing this, is it?" He asked me for an update on how things were unfolding in Ottawa–Vanier. Since his time was very limited, I said, "At some point, Prime Minister, I hope to share with you a full report on what I have experienced." I did not say that I was already keeping a diary. If I had, I expect someone in his office would have come by to insist that I stop.

Later in the evening, first one Ottawa-area Conservative Party MP and then another welcomed me publicly to the "team." And then, at a break in his speech, the Prime Minister singled me out in the crowd to thank me for running and welcomed me as the next member of Parliament for Ottawa–Vanier. That was one heck of an endorsement, likely arranged by one of the many CPC staffers who had crossed paths with me over the last months.

When Marie asked me, upon my returning home, how it went, I had a sober reply: "This is getting serious, Marie!" The PM and the political group in the Ottawa area had endorsed my candidacy, and had done so very publicly. If I felt that I could not let people down before… I felt it much more that day. A rare high among the lows makes it harder to quit every time.

My constant fiddling with the people and personalities who came into and then departed from my core team of supporters always began with a high — when a new volunteer raised my hopes to the level of euphoria — and always ended with a depressing low, when they left. I have already recorded the comings and goings of a few. In all cases, however, I was propelled farther onward by the arrivals than I was ever pulled back by the departures. I owe each and every supporter a great debt. They kept me going.

It began with one of the first to come on board, my brother Gerald, who left for a business opportunity about halfway along. When I despaired about how to make a good showing at the nomination convention and then about how to break into the established ranks of my EDA and the CPC central office, Gerald was a central player on my team.

Gerald, Ross, and one or two others came and went before I was able to count upon Priscilla to go the distance with me as official agent. Carol, Bruce Waverley, Gordon, Guy, and Gene hovered for varying extents of time as possible campaign team leaders, until Luc Savoie stepped forward late in the process at a fundraising event. Luc was an attractive fellow, a politico in his own right, who had run in a municipal election in Quebec City while still a student at Laval University. He was shorter than I was by about two inches (it seems to me that most politicos are short, overweight, or both), pleasant in his features, bilingual, very well read in political and economic theory, and informed about riding issues. By that time I was no longer looking for a campaign manager. Luc would eventually become campaign coordinator. I would learn that he drank far too much Red Bull and experienced the hyperactivity and then near-comatose response that the heavily caffeinated drink imparts. His first act was to sign onto my basic plan for the campaign.

When Luc came forward, he took on the media specialist functions — overseeing brochures and other campaign material, responding to requests for earned media opportunities, and developing and implementing a media outreach plan. While I began to worry early on about the Red Bull, I liked his style and appreciated his background in active politics... though he was not yet thirty years old. We knew some of the same people, including acquaintances way back in Quebec City, where I had also grown up.

Luc's situation, as someone who had recently been with the office of a Quebec City MP sitting with the government as a cabinet minister, raised a new issue that I had not expected to be worrying about so soon: who, among those still with me on voting day, should become part of my office on the Hill if I were to win? As you get closer and closer to election day, you will notice that the stalwarts on your team have begun to wonder about your intentions in this regard. In my case, and I am not proud of it (therefore, consider it a low), I sent out hints to anyone interested that they could count upon a spot. As it happens, my hints were never tested, for two reasons. The first was that I would not win. The second is that most of those who had a vague promise in their back pocket would be gone before election day anyway. Luc was still there, though. He would have had a position with me on the Hill, but I would have required him to leave his Red Bull on the shelf.

Eleanor Brady, who had departed when Carol flew the coop, won my undying gratitude and respect when she returned to the team after Guy departed and said she would now be pleased to stay on as assistant to the office manager and as volunteers coordinator. In her high-energy way, she stayed with me to the end. She would have been a keeper.

The arrivals and departures kept happening, up until the last two weeks. The last to go was Joshua Spence, an energetic and very keen politico who worked for one sitting MP or another. He tried, literally, to muscle me into bringing dozens of telephone staff into my campaign office to make those offensive cold calls that have come to stand for community outreach. We almost came to blows.

A tremendous high came every time I saw that my strategy and tactics for an eventual campaign were falling into place. I was progressively winnowing down what I *needed* to say so that my few seconds with impatient voters resonated with what I would have really *wanted* to say if they had allowed me more time. As I said to Marie one day before she went off to work, "I want my campaign objectives to come down to simple mantras that we can repeat again and again. I want to make it easy for people to distinguish between what I believe this riding needs and what the national office may expect."

The first of these mantras became a simple slogan: "Fifteen years without results is unacceptable," or "Seventy-five years of one-party representation is too long." I foresaw a campaign which used volunteers to deliver the slogan and the "chair" flyer to every home in the riding, a dedicated effort to get signs around the riding, and a competent performance by me in every public appearance opportunity. I assessed that this could be done, plus a brochure mailed out and a few ads placed, well within the minimal budget that I had called for in the basic plan.

As an aside, it is worth noting why something even as innocuous as this simple message could cause a problem for the national office of my party. If I regretted the long-term ownership of the federal seat in my riding by the Liberal Party, and even by the same person, imagine how upset novices must be in most of the Conservative ridings in Alberta and elsewhere in the west! Marie observed that if the Liberal incumbent, furthermore, is a good example of what the CPC like to point to as the worst of what Conservatives in the west think about Liberals in the east (that is, presumptuous, ineffectual), there would be even more reason for the national office not to press too hard on the *Too Long* message.

Another high came each time Marie and I watched a new video from Miriam and Jason, intended for our campaign. The videos got better and better. When we returned home after stopping at their place to see the second (of five overall), I had Amy post it on Facebook and sent copies to the leadership group and some key supporters with my own words of exultant praise. Even then, with what I thought to be a much stronger core team, only Priscilla returned my email. What a gang!

I eventually received comments on the second video from a

party member who had been active in Paul Benoit's campaign a couple of elections earlier. Paul had been the Conservative Party's representative in Ottawa–Vanier immediately after Reform and the Progressive Conservatives had come together under Stephen Harper. In Paul Benoit, the Conservatives appeared to have had the makings of a star: average height, handsome and kind face, friendly manner, a good position in the communications industry, and decidedly conservative orientations toward key symbols like the monarchy. He had done better than any conservative candidate since the riding was created, scoring just under 30% of the vote.

The party member who called me warned, "Mauril will not like the videos!" Her strident advice was to delete and desist. This input was interesting.

I had already observed, with Paul himself and then with a number of other CPC supporters, that Mauril appeared to be quite well liked — but only if you avoided messing with him too directly, and only so long as you stayed in the role of a losing candidate. His smiles and words of encouragement could help to make the journey to defeat a little easier, if you played by his rules. To poke fun at him was verboten, though that, of course, is what I always did. I had no intention of playing things Mauril's way.

Late one afternoon, over coffee and scones at The Scone Witch, down the street from where I live, I met with Paul Benoit again. My interest was to learn more about the Liberal team I would be up against. I wanted to know if they were people to be concerned about if I pressed too hard. After almost eighty years of Liberal hold on this riding, the number of people in all income strata who depended upon the Liberal incumbent's influence was doubtlessly very high, beginning with the dozen or so in Mauril's own office.

Paul's answer to that question was "no," but not without qualification. Liberal party activists in Ottawa–Vanier, it appeared, get hot under the collar with residents who do not stay loyal to the Liberal cause.

I would be finding this out for myself when, at a supper to salute new Canadians of Congolese origin, the wife of the man who had invited Marie and me was left crying after what appeared to be a friendly hug from one of Mauril's supporters. I learned this again when the editor of a community newspaper was driven out of a social event for having published my letter critical of the self-indulgence among the Liberal cohort of federal, provincial, and municipal career politicians. When the editor of a regional paper abruptly left his position after the second of my letters was published, I had my suspicions. When small-business owners enthusiastically put my signs up in the windows of their establishments and those signs were replaced by Liberal signs within a couple of days, I wondered.

Paul — like the person who had called me — would have had me meet the Liberal incumbent on his terms. Those terms began with Mr. Bélanger's proclivity to keep public discussion during past elections focused upon local issues, perhaps borne of the many years when Liberals were in power. In those days he may have needed to dodge his government's positions on federal issues.

On Mauril's three main issues, for example, I found the incumbent's analysis to be weak, his facts to be incomplete or wrong, and his perspective to be municipal or provincial rather than federal, as it should have been. His three main issues, which had not changed in sixteen years, were the future of a now-closed air force base around the corner from my home in Rockcliffe, the location of a new bridge over the Ottawa River from the Quebec side to reduce traffic through the middle of Ottawa–Vanier, and the reduction of traffic flow — especially trucks — down King Edward Avenue that cut through the heart of our most densely populated district.

I would develop my own sense of what the developed site of a former air force base in our riding might look like, but I always emphasized that the federal interest was exclusively to sell lands which had become surplus to federal requirement in order to reduce the federal budget deficits. I would elaborate upon my own preferred location for a new bridge across the Ottawa River, but I would lead my interventions with the reminder that the federal interest was engaged exclusively because the river itself was in federal jurisdiction. I worked with expert colleagues at CRG Consulting to design and cost my own solutions to traffic congestion on King Edward Street but said publicly that the federal interest would be engaged only if the City wanted to draw from Action Canada funds to help pay for a reconstruction.

To deal with those issues on Mauril's terms would have required me to acknowledge that he was right to keep placing them front and centre before voters at every election, and right to attest that only he could be trusted to find solutions. I dared to ask, "After sixteen years, what is it about the ineptness of that man that has prevented him from correctly identifying the federal interest and from directing the provincial and municipal governments toward solutions?" For eleven of those sixteen years, Mr. Bélanger's party had been in power, and he had himself been an associate minister of National Defence when the future of Canadian Forces Base Rockcliffe got so badly mangled.

I said to Paul that I would counter Mauril's platform with the observation that correct management of the political process, beginning with an accurate understanding of government jurisdictions, is the only way to achieve results. I observed again, firmly, that Mauril had not done a good job. He had not delivered. It was very clear from his replies that Paul thought Mauril had been a very good MP indeed and could be judged a mighty success by the quality of his newsletters alone.

I answered that Mauril's newsletters, if anyone ever stopped to read them, echo Liberal Party messaging from the Hill and say almost nothing new for the riding. Given that he'd had the same priority list of riding issues for the past sixteen years, how could they? I added that if all his newsletters since his first election in

1995 dealt only with the training of his dog, he would still have won all the subsequent elections. He owed his place to political inertia in the riding, I said, not to performance. To label this late-afternoon coffee a low would be to rate its impact upon me too highly. It was depressing.

Perhaps the worst of the lows began to rumble through my political life when I raised with my core team — as it then still was — how to tackle the list of names of people who had property signs during the previous election. I recounted in chapter 2 how I wanted us to call them all, confirm interest in their doing this again, and then drop by their homes to say hello and welcome a short discussion. When we dropped by, we could get the signed endorsements I would need in order to become legal when an election was called. Also, we could use the list of confirmed names for lawn signs to call people up personally when we hosted our upcoming Christmas-season event for volunteers.

I was impatient to get on with these tasks, I said, because — as always — an election could be called at any time and I needed to be ready with my ground game.

All I got in return, except from Priscilla, were stares of incomprehension. Eventually I would be able to achieve most of what I had hoped to achieve when I first raised this challenge, but all the contacting would be done by me (70%), Priscilla (20%), and my daughter (10%). Guy and Gene said they would rather quit. No one else had the time.

Meanwhile, we continued to walk door to door.

It did not help me that the EDA remained convinced, throughout our time together, that DVC, Voter ID, and GOTV were the way to go. It did not help either that the EDA and the party wanted me to repeat again and again, at one door and to one human contact after another, the "three big ideas" that our party wanted to be known for centrally. In my case, it was "tough on crime," "good for the economy," and "strong support for the military." And in my case, those slogans did not help me nearly as much as the Liberal and NDP candidates were helped by what they shouted in their turn: "Don't trust the Conservatives."

As a novice candidate, one whose background had prepared me to engage in substantive exchanges, the slogans were an embarrassment. I never used them. Earlier in this book, when talking about the test of values, I elaborated upon my determination to engage residents in a meaningful exchange of views. When on someone's doorstep I was asked about "tough on crime," a slogan that was being repeated daily by party leaders on Parliament Hill anyway, I would use the question to open a discussion on actual crime rates in various parts of our riding, and I would ask what additional preventative and intervention steps a resident would like to see governments take. I did not want, after my thirty years in the military, in the public sector, and as a consultant, to close out my career with sloganeering. Often enough, doors would be opened by people I had met professionally or personally at some stage in my life. Novices such as I knock on doors because we believe we have something to offer. We do not want to be remembered as people who have lost our minds.

On the issue of crime, by the way, the CPC slogan was unhelpful because the crime that happened in the more troubled neighbourhoods in my riding was very local, relatively petty (break-and-enter, among neighbours), and endemic only among youth. To tackle crime of this kind with too much vehemence would be to tear apart the families who worried as much about the future of their kids as the police did. We needed more social programs, which come from the provincial level, and more leadership at all political levels. In my opinion, candidates have to understand the dynamics involved and lead with feelings of sympathy and empathy rather than revenge.

When I was asked about the ways in which contemporary media and the government hotlines might make a difference, I joined my interlocutors in their reaction of despair. "The police never come," was a lament I often heard in the Centretown and Overbrook districts of the riding.

Where at one time reporting a crime required the physical effort of going to the police detachment or waiting on the line for ringing phones to be answered, today it is as easy as typing a few lines onto a form on the Internet or dialling 911. A police department spokesman in the detachment on McArthur Road explained that the number of police was not going to go up. As the number of incoming messages increased in leaps and bounds, the rate of police response, as a necessary consequence, was going to keep plunging. Even as real crime went down, the appearance of crime going up was certain to be reinforced.

In that small percentage of time with potential voters when our interaction included discourse about politics such as my exchanges about crime, I am convinced that my capacity to engage in informed debate made a difference. I am convinced that the multiplier effect, the factor of twenty that the Honourable Stockwell Day had talked about at a breakfast organized by my association, went into high gear after I moved on to the next house, the next apartment door, or the next local business. My ability to persuade people was always a high for me, and always impressed EDA members and the students who had been recruited by party headquarters to help our EDA deliver its silly programs. But again and again, my EDA and party representatives tried to shut me down. The low quickly followed each time I was told that I spent too long at the doors.

"Remember," I would be told, "your chance of being elected in this riding has very little to do with who you are." By now I was reading widely in the literature on electoral politics and already knew that the results obtained by a candidate in a federal or provincial election these days are explained over 95% by central party messaging and under 5% by the candidate. The influence from the centre can even be as much as 100%. This was the case for just about all candidates elected in Quebec who represented Canada's "grassroots" New Democratic Party in the 2011 federal election.

Yet I still believed that I could make it different.

Months after my last failed attempt at a "Let's Talk Politics" event (when my EDA had dropped the ball), and now in the thick of the election, I tried again. The event was scheduled for Café Caco, the Portuguese community's place, which by this time I had made my regular haunt for coffees and lunches. At the last minute the national CPC office asked Luc, whom I had exhorted to organize the event, to cancel, and he did, without asking me. Notwithstanding my performance over the preceding eighteen months, during which I had even been asked by party headquarters to stand in for a sitting MP to debate Middle East issues before a decidedly hostile audience, the party still did not trust me, as an experienced person, to handle myself appropriately before an audience of interested citizens and possibly a few journalists.

I had already gone ahead and ordered food for the event. I went with Marie and Priscilla. We invited all those present at the café that night to enjoy the trays of delights Priscilla had already paid for, and we had a great evening. Not a word was said about politics, not even by me. This night was a high because of the resilience of the three of us: my wife, Priscilla, and me. It was a low because of what the absence of interested voters said about the state of politics. Political parties are not anxious to draw members of the public into an uncontrolled situation where talking about politics is the objective of their candidates.

If democracy is to become more vibrant in our society, citizens' courage to talk politics in private and public settings must grow. But to talk politics is to risk disagreement and debate. Political parties worry that candidates who expound upon different points of view will instead foment discord. I believe they also worry — and rightly so — that far too many citizens have set aside, have lost, or are no longer educated in the skills of dialogue. We constantly hear about the imperative for schools and universities in Canada to ramp up training in business and innovation. The disciplines associated with rhetoric and elocution, key though they may be for healthy democracies, are never mentioned.

One cold winter morning, January 12, I had a coffee with the *Ottawa Citizen*'s Randall Denley, to whom I had reached out because I enjoyed reading his two novels — one of which touched upon politics. To my mind, the discussion between us went very well. He was much less interested in my view about issues nationally, regionally, or locally than I expected, however. His interest was clearly in my person as a candidate — my reasons for running, my experiences to date, and my expectations for the future.

I would soon learn that Randall was himself considering a run for public office, at the provincial level. While he was already closely associated with the political process because of his regular commentary about politics in his column in the Postmedia papers, he would be a novice candidate in the way I use the phrase. Randall had the makings of an excellent member of the provincial legislature. (He would go on to run twice in the riding of Ottawa Centre. He would lose both times, to a politico belonging to the Liberal Party who had been in politics for his entire life. Randall would be taken down by central messaging out of his party's headquarters in Toronto.)

The CPC would not have wanted my freewheeling discussion with Randall Denley to take place. That is why I did not share the news of it with the national office. Should an article on me come out in the local paper, I said to myself, I will stumble upon an excuse of some kind. If the reaction to anything I do is stridently negative and the party wants me out... I will quit.

Meanwhile, life went on. Along the way I was jolted by a story that appeared in the national newspaper, the *Globe and Mail*, regarding CRG Consulting. The company I was an associate vice-president with had been caught up in a bid-rigging "scandal." There was a risk that a link would be made between me and the company. The high I had experienced when the president of CRG Consulting had welcomed my continuing use of my title in public settings now dived toward the possible low of being taken down by EDA members who had long ago begun to resent my independent approach.

I shared my understanding of CRG's predicament with the national office that very day. To my great satisfaction and surprise, the response from party headquarters was immediate: nothing to worry about. They understood that an associate VP is a separate legal entity from the firm itself. If an attempt were made to give profile to CRG, to the firm's problems, and to my being on the firm's executive, I thought, this might actually help rather than hinder my cause. It would make the point that the firm I was associated with had been a serious player. That is why our firm was targeted among the many that behave in business in the same way that CRG had been called out for. Bad news is always better than no news.

For his part, the president of the firm, Brian Card, and his principals were comfortable about the risk that a public link to me and my role with the CPC would give more profile to their problem than they might otherwise expect. Indeed, Brian added that CRG Consulting was planning to build a new line of business in the area of Aboriginal affairs and that I would be his first choice to lead this venture after the upcoming election if I did not win. He would keep the position open until then.

So at CRG Consulting, my executive table seat would be held open for me. This was both a high, because of its being a confidence boost, and a destabilizer for my perseverance. There would be many times in the months ahead that a safe landing among senior consultants and executives I had come to know and like a great deal seemed awfully attractive.

On one of those days when I mused about stepping down, Colin McSweeny, the guy at party headquarters responsible for the performance of all EDAs and candidates in eastern Ontario, said to Marie in my presence, "What else does he have to do?" It felt to both of us like a bit of an insult.

Given my professional background, I knew I could have figured something out even if the CRG offer had not been in my hand. In contrast, in the case of most of the politicos I have encountered — including our riding's MP — that question would be a difficult one to answer. Politics is all they have ever known.

But I had been working as the candidate for over a year by this point. I had become determined to stay on the political journey, to continue to take the highs and the lows of it, until the journey was over. If Colin had asked "What else does he *want* to do?" I would have answered, "Nothing."

It would be misleading, however, to suggest that my determination and my resolve remained always strong. The right disincentive, at the right time and in the right place, could still have had its effect. I had already learned a heck of a lot. After more than a year, I already had a story to tell about the political process — one that I believed might be important.

I recall a quiet few hours in late fall, moving lazily from the deck at our cottage on Sharbot Lake to the little beach area, then past the dock and our new bowrider to the pumphouse at the far end of the lakeshore. I took note of all the projects I was not doing because almost all of my waking time was by then devoted to political activities.

I wondered, did I really care enough about politics to do the job of an elected member of Parliament if I were successful? But I also knew that quitting was no longer an option. I would not let myself and others down by walking away in a huff. I would have to be sent packing because of a clash between my principles and my party's imperatives... a clash that never came.

I remember on that day picking up a forty-year-old text I have on the subject of Bakunin and anarchist political theory, and this helped a bit. I became a conservative in my undergraduate years, when I stood with Edmund Burke in his admonishment of

Thomas Paine in their exchange of letters during the French Revolution at the end of the eighteenth century. Burke's perspectives on liberty had led me to the anarchists (not the violent ones!). Anarchist theory has always stood for me as the dreamy vision of a society where small government is taken all the way to no government. The goal of the political theorists and politicians I have favoured has typically been to guide societies toward a future where life can be enjoyed by and be productive for as many of our fellow human beings as possible, with as little interference from people of influence and power as can be managed.

Productive to what end, of course, is the conundrum. For some (monks in silent retreats) it is okay to promote lifestyles which manifestly cannot be enjoyed until the afterlife. For me, life on earth is a journey (much larger and longer than my current political round) which provides eyes and ears to the eternal God. We are all a part of the "forever," and our chance to make a personal contribution while on this earth is a privilege we should make the most of.

So I would carry on for reasons based in personal motives and ethics and also for reasons based in theory and belief. If I were to win the upcoming election, I knew I would serve well and productively. If I were to lose, I would continue to focus upon the wonder of living and make my ongoing contributions from a place back in the ranks of CRG executives or from the sidelines.

Because my journey had already lasted longer than I had expected, I told myself in February 2011 that I should reconsider what to do if there no election appeared on the horizon. We had expected one, from one month to the next, for the past fifteen months. The test of endurance, in my case, seemed to be having no end in sight.

A logical breaking point would come for me in March 2011, if the government passed its budget and looked like it could carry on for another two years. That would be a good time to resign as candidate and run instead for a position on the board of the EDA, at its next annual general meeting. (The association's constitution does not allow an executive member of the board to also be the association's candidate.) From a position on the board, with a plan to eventually run for president, I would stay involved in the politics of the day. I would also be able to support the incoming candidate who replaced me by handing over the great many files of information and talking points I had pulled together.

By doing this, I would confirm to the association and to the party that I could be counted upon. Within the world of political organizers, I would likely be seen to have stepped up a rung on the ladder rather than down — especially given that a Conservative is so unlikely to win in Ottawa–Vanier anyway. As I have said in a previous chapter, more novices like me need to get engaged in politics at the ground level, not just as candidates.

Marie, needless to say, was enthusiastic when I shared these musing with her. In reply, she offered herself to a future in which she would support me just as fervently and consistently as board member of the electoral district association as she had supported my journey so far. The EDA would have seen two novices join the ranks, not just one.

In the end, and to Marie's disappointment, every time that I mused about the alternatives in this way, I rediscovered my resolve to carry on shortly after. "I am everything a proper candidate should be," I would say. "I am credible and I have a team solidly in place. I have only a few loose ends to tie up. We are ready to go." To say these words would affirm that I was at a high in the process. To see Marie's discouraged look in reply would be a low. To experience the next deep low that almost immediately followed every high of recommitment meant for me that the test of endurance would go on until the day of the vote.

CHAPTER 7.

THE TEST OF ISOLATION

Isolation is both a word and a feeling. It connotes loneliness, but not necessarily. Within communities it implies that a particular person or group is avoided or shunned. As one of the tests in the gauntlet, it means the person running for public office must move further and further out of his or her comfort zone of people and of contexts. The people include spouses, children, friends, and business associates. The contexts are family, neighbourhoods, and the place of work.

In the chapters that relate to the other tests, especially the test of endurance, you have already seen how my political journey brought about the severance of multiple relationships and a necessary disengagement from my profession and place of work. In my diary of my journey, I kept a record of tensions that grew within my immediate and extended family as the weeks and months wore on. If I ever send Prime Minister Harper a copy of my diary, I may leave out many of these personal details. Long-time friends parted company, my welcome in neighbourhood organizations became less, new people who came into my topsy-turvy life as enthusiastic volunteers departed when other opportunities came up, or sometimes in a huff.

Upon reflection, I liken what happened to a transformation. Running through the gauntlet transforms the private person into a public person.

Every aspect of privacy that you had come to take for granted, including home and email addresses, is moved into the public sphere. Your privacy is given up. You willingly expose your values. You commit your family and close friends to the venture in order to get the support you need. You cast aside EDA members who question your presumption when you feel the imperative of assuming leadership of your own campaign. For reasons of self-preservation as your run continues, your focus upon yourself gets more exclusive.

I learned with regard to the test of isolation that what happened to me happens to most candidates. When I complained about the performance of others, the president of my EDA and the CPC point man for all EDAs in eastern Ontario both charged me with not being ruthless enough. I was told that few candidates have the same manager at the end of a political campaign as they had at the start. The transformation from private to public person is, to use the words of Willy Loman's wife in *Death of a Salesman*, "a casting off."

If you are staring an opportunity to run for public office in the face, therefore, take a while to rethink why you believe yourself ready to do this.

It is extremely important to understand at the front end where things stand with your partner or spouse, your adult children, your extended families, your friends, your neighbours, and your professional colleagues. For the whole time that you are preparing for an eventual election, and then even more during the election itself, you will have to devote your intelligence and your wit — to say nothing about your patience and your health — to your own situation. If you have been counted upon by those closest to you to help keep a lid on family tensions and feuding, know that during your period as a candidate you will fall down in this role.

Ask yourself if you are ready to become identified by one and all with the party you will step out publicly for. No matter how solid your reputation has become over your years as a private citizen in your community, no matter how carefully you have guarded your private thoughts among close friends and within your own family, to step out into the public eye with a political party brand on your forehead is to be typecast for the duration of your candidacy and, in the eyes of many, for the rest of your life.

If you are taking this step without the enthusiastic support of your partner or spouse, you should sit with him or her and be honest about what lies ahead. You may not be able to build up his or her enthusiasm, but it will be imperative to build up understanding. It would help, for example, to share this book.

No matter how supportive your immediate family is, no matter how united they want to be with you, there will come times when you risk their stepping away. The longer your run lasts, the greater the risk. Even for you, the well-being and future of your public person will become more important than the private person you were at the outset. Toward the end of your run, you are likely to find yourself referring to "the candidate" in the third person, just like everyone else.

Look at what often happens to first-time candidates, both novices and politicos, when they win. The winners leave their private lives back home in order to take up public life in Ottawa or a provincial capital. Marriages break up. Children lose one of their principal anchors and go off the rails. Public friends and public romances displace the colleagues and lovers who were there before.

Politicos come from families and backgrounds where coping with these changes has become par for the course. The Clintons stay married. For novices, though, it can be devastating… as well as embarrassing.

Remember: novices usually lose. This means that you are highly unlikely to leave your private life behind for very long. Whatever you have cast off during your time as a candidate must be reckoned with when you step back into the world you would have left behind had you won.

Much of how my transformation from private to public person played out has already been described. By the day of the vote, nineteen months after I had submitted my name to the Ottawa–Vanier EDA as a possible candidate, the team around me was a very different group of people than it had been a year and a half before.

It shocks me still to read the list of names of people I welcomed when they joined up and then regretted when they departed — Carol Latimer, Gordon Peters, Mark Rogal, Heather Parks, Ross Carrothers, Gene Pierce, Guy DesRoches, Bruce Waverley, Wendy Shore, Brock Stephens, Shaun Warren, Robert Sampson, Jack and Mary Darlington, Colin Lindley, my brother Gerald, my daughters Amy and Robin, and others.

Very few EDA members were part of the revamped campaign team coordinated by Luc Savoie. The greatest number were young politicos from the Hill who had been sent by their various MP offices to spend their five weeks of unemployment (assuming re-election) helping out a local candidate.

The departure of a few of those listed had very little to do with their attitude toward me. My brother had other business. My friend since public school, Colin Lindley, had a vacation opportunity during the election that he could not reasonably set aside. Their cases make the point that, whereas I as candidate was being transformed from a private to a public person, for those two and a number of others, their private lives remained much more important than any desire to hitch themselves to my trajectory. And good for them. They made the right choice.

The story of two of my three daughters is important enough to bear a moment's reflection. Those three young women were the three little girls who remained with their mother when she and I separated some twenty-five years before. My marriage to Marie, with the addition of our two boys, Kees and Gerrit, landed all of us in a family of seven who spent alternate weekends and a month in the summer all together. As the centrepiece in this blended family, I, as father, had a duty that I had always acquitted myself of very well. I love all my kids. I wanted, and Marie wanted, that the five of them saw as little distance between each other as possible. The words "half" or "step" were never spoken alongside "brother" or "sister" among them.

During eighteen of my nineteen months as a candidate, I had the strong support of Amy, support from Robin when she was in town, and the enthusiastic participation of Miriam and her partner. My transformation to a public life, however, allowed me less and less time to achieve the bits of reconciliation required when small acts caused hurts that I would ordinarily have addressed immediately. I was now much more concerned about hurts to myself.

When Marie read my diary after the election, she could see that I had done what I could to continue wrestling with upsets among us. The management of Facebook content had been a particular irritant. Amy did not like my having asked Marie to act as a clearing house for content that Amy and I developed between us. Marie, for her part, did not like the loss of control that inappropriate content on the Internet could bring. My dancing between my eldest daughter and my wife became more inept as the months wore on. The explosion came just two days into the period of the writ.

When I sat on the stage at a local high school for the first of a half-dozen public debates, in a large auditorium filled with a couple of hundred spectators, my mind was troubled by an exchange of emails I had read that very morning. I did not do well in that first debate. First Amy and then Robin made the point — very clearly — that I had failed them. I had not provided the support they had come to expect, and they wanted nothing more to do with me.

And so it would be until my private life was restored. After my loss in the election, all of us had the time we needed to rejig what we expected from one another. We eventually got to the other end successfully and became a stronger family as a result.

I wonder, would we have done, had I won? Is it possible to have a public life devoted to others and still be a rounded person who has time for all things private? I have to hope so. Had I won, I hope that the maturity which comes with a successful and varied career would have equipped me to restore the balance needed for good mental health.

In one of the many rounds of introspection recorded in my diary, I wrote about the day when I was troubled more than usual by the realization that life is short.

> I am well aware that my dad is gone. My mother, at 93, fell and broke her hip two weeks previously. The dog is getting old, Marie's mom and most of her mom's family are now passed away. Marie's dad is 84. When I meet with the young people on my new EDA team, and when the political veterans I meet are 20 years younger than I am, I realize how far along the treadmill I have moved.
>
> I deal with thoughts like these by realizing that we are all in the same boat, all of us who are alive — including the flora and the fauna. For all I know the stones, minerals and metals themselves are part of infinity's endless evolution and may be headed to a round of consciousness (aided and abetted by us?) that will replace our own self-awareness a few million years from now.
>
> When one tries to grasp the endlessness of time, it is oddly comforting to know that one's physical components are likely permanent, one's physical reality will always be part of the firmament, and one's awareness may always shine through the awareness of family... and possibly the awareness of spirit. Nothing can be ruled out. But one's physical presence is certain to be part of the universe forever.
>
> What I owe to the universe, I think, is to make profitable use of my own time as a self-aware life form. I know I have always tried to do that.
>
> I think my present journey raises the bar. If I do not win the next election, though, it may truly be time for me to "retire." My parting contribution to politics will be to oversee the resolution of financial issues that may remain from my campaign and thereafter to remain

active in politics — if at all — only from a distance. My most important job will be to focus upon the remarkable miracle my own life represents.

As Raymond Chrétien, with whom I worked quite closely on one of my bigger contracts with CRG Consulting, said to me at a reception held by his law firm in Montreal this past Christmas, "Rem, at some point we have to get ready." He meant that we have to prepare for the world hereafter, and I agree. I think one gets ready by slowly sloughing off the need to be an individual who triumphs over others. I think one begins, if married, by melding more effectively with one other person, then also with the family (kids, grandkids), but also with the community at large. It will be very satisfying if I can lose myself in others long before I lose myself.

When I reread those words now in light of what is said about the test of isolation and what has been written about the human spirit (Ralph Heintzman, *Rediscovering Reverence*, 2011), I wonder what winning would have done to me. I expect I would have set aside my private self for the duration of my time in public life. I could well have lost my private self altogether, but the higher purpose would not have been spiritual. I would have returned to what was left for me in the private sphere among family, friends, and business colleagues at the end of my time in politics and tried to pick up the pieces. Because my journey into active politics was short, picking up the pieces was not so difficult. I was lucky.

CHAPTER 8.

THE TEST OF ACCOMPLISHMENT

The final test in the gauntlet is the test of accomplishment. Will you be able to achieve that which you set out to do? Will you get to the finish line in the way that you intended? This test awaits you when you have run through all the others.

After having passed by or through all the other tests, this final one is the ultimate determiner of whether you enter public office or get kicked back to where you came from. And if that weren't pressure enough, on top of that, all the previous tests come at you all over again with renewed immediacy during an intense five-week period called the election. This test is whipped out at you when the writ drops, and then only if you are still leaping or limping along.

Except at bedtime, during the election period your privacy is gone. Every day will be a test of your values, either in the ways you display them on the public stage or in how you explain them to the myriad of journalists and bloggers who ask you questions. By now all of your own resources have been committed and have sorted themselves out one way or another. Your control over your own destiny has been transferred into the contents of a campaign plan of your own design, over which your official agent now has full control because of how she controls the money. You have almost gone the distance. Once you are fully into this last test, only serious illness or death will be the legal off-ramps that permit someone else to step into your place for a rescheduled election in your riding. You have become "the candidate" even in your own eye.

The novice and the politico are very differently positioned for this last test.

If you — like I — started running the gauntlet a long time ago, the repeat of all the tests during the five weeks of an election will not be a big deal. You have wrestled with each of those tests before, often in excruciating circumstances and sometimes with painful results. You have wrung every ounce of menace out of them. On the day the election is called, you will still have a couple of days to reconfirm that everything is in place. You must be ready. For me, these two days were the most intense of all.

To be legal as a candidate running for public office, you need to table with elections officials (Elections Canada, in my case) the names of your official agent and your official auditor. If you are representing a recognized federal or provincial party, you will also need to have the leader of your party confirm your status to those same elections officials. Your party will want to know who your campaign manager is going to be, because political staffers at headquarters will not want to deal with you directly. They will work on the assumption that your campaign manager is totally in charge. Remember the slogan: the candidate who manages his or her own campaign is a fool.

If you have been successful in bringing a shadow team increasingly into the picture while your EDA still ruled the day, now is the time for your own team to step forward. The EDA will beat a retreat for the five weeks of the campaign. If your EDA is in a capital city and its members include staffers who work for sitting politicians, most of them are going to leave town. Their jobs in the House of Commons or in provincial legislatures have come to a temporary end. If they had been trusted by you to tidy everything up before handing things over to your campaign team, you must expect that they will drop the ball. Their new priority is to work on the campaigns of their respective political bosses. The

EDA essentially dissolves for the duration of the campaign. You must expect the dissolution to begin in the week *before* the writ is actually dropped.

To move quickly when the writ drops, you may, as I did, need still more money. You have to set up those signs with your name on them (Vote for Me!). During the weeks when election fever is starting to build in earnest, therefore, you will need to have set up a campaign bank account (most banks have a branch officer who is familiar with how this done). In their dwindling enthusiasm, your EDA will have had to sign the contracts which produce four hundred lawn signs and a hundred arterial signs, the ones that stand along the main streets in town and along the highways.

Your designated official agent will be the person most likely to help you get your EDA to deliver on the lawn signs. The EDA must also sign the lease for your campaign office. To leave the location of an office and the transactions involved (including setting up telephones, renting office equipment, and acquiring basic office necessities) to the first hours of the period of the writ will land you the least attractive available space. Prior to the writ being dropped, only the EDA is legally positioned to do any of this. The draw on the EDA bank account for these items (signs, office lease, and office equipment and supplies) will be about $20,000. If your EDA has only $30,000 in the bank, as mine did, it means only $10,000 in cash will be transferred to your campaign bank account.

Your official agent will be the person most concerned (aside from you) about finding where your EDA finance officer has run off to when the writ drops. You have to get any leftover EDA funds (after money for the signs and office lease have either been paid or set aside) into your campaign team bank account as soon as you can. Indeed, your official agent will be the most important person in your life not only for the five weeks of the election, but for a month or two afterward as well.

Unless you are happy to run desperately from pillar to post starting day one of the election period, there is a long list of other items that will have to be ready in advance. Given your background and your need to keep your reputation intact, I am sure you will have given those other items as much thought as I did.

If you want to stay ahead of national office instructions, make sure your campaign literature — customized for your riding — is ready, in the order of a thousand copies of each flyer and brochure. Prepare for a cost of $500 for each item, and prepare for the hoped-for possibility that many more thousands of copies will be needed because — in principle — every residence in your riding should get one of each. If you do not trust your team of supporters to be numerous enough to make much of a dent in a riding of, say, 60,000 residences, prepare in advance for a "direct mail" by Canada Post of 60,000 one-page "doorknockers." The cost for this will be just under $12,000.

In order to create a serious impression upon readers of local newspapers, you should have, ready to roll, advertisements which will get your name, face, and key messages into the public eye at least once each week of the campaign. Assuming there are three regional and local papers in your area, read by people in their homes or places of work, twelve advertisements (in French and English, for the Ottawa area) will cost your campaign another $6,000.

Your fellow first-time candidates, especially the ones I call the politicos, are highly unlikely to have prepared themselves at all. They know what to expect. They will play catch-up with the imperatives of an election campaign after the campaign begins. Their campaign literature will be obtained by buying into templates developed by the national or provincial party they represent. They will allow their campaigns to build up debt (likely owed to themselves or their families) in the hope that public subsidies at the end of the campaign will be adequate to cover those debts. Politicos are basically along for the ride. They may hope — as you do — that they will be elected, but, as I have said before, their futures do not depend on it. Their reputations are enhanced by the mere fact of having put themselves into the ring. Your reputation, on the other hand, is at high risk of being diminished.

When you review the items and the costs just set out, you will see that a bare-bones campaign will require at least $50,000. This is the amount that has to be committed, if not physically paid, by the time the first week of the campaign is over. Your official agent cannot commit to any expenditure without knowing that the funds required will be available, so almost without doubt, you or your family will have to make a personal loan to the campaign. The key to how much lies in the amount of cash your EDA was able to transfer to the campaign team bank account.

If you have set the stage for a personal loan, you will, of course, be running not only to keep your reputation intact, but also to protect your bank account.

The phase shift that happens to you on the day the writ drops (but only after your party leader has confirmed your status as official candidate) is that your EDA is no longer in business as a champion of your party's brand. You and your official agent are together in business as champions for your cause, which is to get elected. You will continue to champion the brand, of course. But the very best you can do for your party on this concluding round is to get yourself elected... without damaging the chances of any other party candidate by what you may say or do.

By the end of the first week of the campaign, you will find that a much larger campaign team has begun to assemble around you than you ever expected. There are party supporters in your riding who wanted to have nothing to do with your EDA but who enjoy becoming active during the short weeks of a campaign. Believe it or not — and it's hard to believe given how tough it was to get help prior to the election call — people will stop by your office on the very first day it is open and ask what they can do to help. My campaign coordinator had his hands full directing volunteers to the various functions that needed to be performed. My campaign team leaders, primarily Luc and Eleanor (with Marie always in reserve), needed to keep everyone happy during the five weeks that constituted the test of accomplishment.

A typical campaign team, within a week of the election call, will have within its ranks a volunteers coordinator, a public relations manager, an office administration group, community outreach people, and so on. While you would have been lucky to see more than a dozen people at a meeting of your shadow team prior to the writ being dropped, a campaign team meeting at the start of week two of your campaign will need space for at least fifty people. It is best to hold such meetings over a lunch hour or supper because many of those folk enjoy the sandwiches and pizzas, and the campaign gossip, which flow easily over pop during the day or beers in the evening. By the end of the campaign, the care and feeding of your team will have added another $5,000 to your costs.

Your party and the politicos running in ridings which border your own will have known all along that campaign activity begins to happen, almost regardless of pre-writ preparations, in the days immediately after the writ drops. This is one of the reasons why, when you kept pressing for results during those long and lonely months before the election was called, you were a curiosity for your EDA and your party.

Any number of things can go wrong in the first two weeks of your campaign. By now you will have reworked your campaign plan dozens of times. The structure, financing, and early days of campaign operations have been rendered in fine detail. Be very sure that the core group of your shadow team understands that the script must be respected. Not many on your team will have your professional background. Not many will appreciate the importance of discipline when people run enthusiastically out of the gate.

Many of those who step forward and become volunteers during weeks one and two will want your campaign to conform to the standard operating procedures they became familiar with in previous campaigns. You will need the help of your core team to keep these new folks under control. The preponderant position of your official agent will be key. Your official agent must approve every document that is made public. Your official agent controls the money. Nothing can be done without the official agent's approval or without the money.

If you have determined upon an approach in your campaign that suits your personal style rather than mimicks what all of the politicos will be doing, you must be prepared for tensions throughout the election period. Those tensions will mostly come between core team members and the volunteers who showed up unexpectedly. Those volunteers will include a number of experienced politicos who will listen more to party headquarters than to you.

Again, the surest way to control what actually happens on the ground is by controlling the money. By denying funds to any and every activity that does not fit into your campaign plan, your official agent can shut down initiatives like the inevitable call for dozens of telephones, to be staffed by four dozen volunteers, to phone the thousands of names in your party's information management system. Your official agent can deny the funds needed in advance to buy into flyers and brochures built upon official party templates in which you will see all kinds of messaging that make no sense in your riding. (You will also see, if you look very closely at those templates, that your picture is supposed to appear somewhere below that of your party leaders and of any politicians in your area who already hold seats in the legislature.)

Your official agent will become greatly disliked. My campaign coordinator, who was bombarded on one side by party headquarters staff, had a hell of a time controlling the urge of newly recruited volunteers to do what they had always done before. Poor Luc was handcuffed by Priscilla to the imperatives set out in my basic plan. My communications team became frustrated because my advertisements had been ready to go for months and my media lines had long been ready in both French and English. They too had precious little to do. Our material was already out there. Calling back the advertisements that Priscilla and I had prearranged to run in weeks three, four, and five of the campaign was not an option. Everyone blamed Priscilla.

By the end of week two, however, if you have stayed the course, your team will begin to hum. It takes about fourteen days for your army of new volunteers to be pruned of those who would rather work on the standard model. The ones who stay will begin to appreciate working on the basis of a plan that is customized to the riding they are in. You will see confirmed what you learned in your business environment before politics: almost everyone enjoys the satisfaction of results intended and results achieved. Almost everyone appreciates a professional approach. Most people in your new army will love working on an "old-style" campaign where the focus is upon meeting people, talking substance, being honest and on topic. Dispensing with the meaningless busywork in the "science" of electoral politics is as good for their souls as it was for your own.

Unless the pizza and beer are of very high quality, not a single volunteer enjoys sitting with others behind a bank of telephones and computers to make cold calls or send bulk messages that upset the recipients 100% of the time. No one really enjoys the science part of it very much.

Your party, by the way, will try very hard to get your campaign manager to devote as much volunteer time as possible to the data-gathering exercise. National and provincial party headquarters will have pressed your campaign manager to install those dozens of telephones I mentioned before. They have totally accepted that success in elections depends upon what is done centrally rather than locally. Party headquarters have fully embraced the finding that you as a candidate cannot make more than 5% of the difference in the final tally of votes.

If they had to choose, party headquarters would rather you use the period of the election to build up data on Voter ID than spend your time vying for votes on the streets, in the homes, and in the businesses of your riding. Voter ID is a very expensive program in terms of volunteers, time and money. If your campaign team uses most of its time and most of its money to improve party records, the resulting improvement will be subsidized — up to 60% of costs — when the campaign is over. In your case, the aficionados of Voter ID in party headquarters would be grateful for this outcome. Since they expect you to lose anyway, why not build toward a better future?

With accurate data on the voting intention of all residents (names, telephone numbers, email addresses), the GOTV program could one day be implemented all across the country or a province out of a central office. The best-organized party could then have a real chance of winning no matter who the candidate happens to be or what he or she does. But what kind of future is that? What does it say about democracy in Canada that this kind of future is not entirely a fantasy?

One of the activities that remained high on my preferred list throughout the period of the election was participation in public debates. I was very confident in my ability to do a good job in these. You will find, however, that your party does not like activities of this kind. There are at least two reasons for this, the validity of both being a matter that should be of growing concern to us all.

The first reason is that a growing number of first-time candidates for public office are politicos with weak professional backgrounds. In public debate, most candidates, therefore, do not impress very much. They learned as young aspirants to limit what they say to slogans. In their gathered number on public stages and media channels across the land, their performance and their antics dumb down the political process. Party elites are intuitively aware that their hold on power depends upon the political system remaining in high enough repute to ensure wide regard for the powers they wield. Party leaders and their staff do not like seeing the reality of politics — that it has become a world of politicos — displayed too openly.

Another reason why more and more candidates are being told by their party headquarters to absent themselves from public forums is that, for the most part, the people who make up the audience are already committed to one candidate or another. Public forums at one time, and perhaps still at the municipal level, could be about meeting the candidates and could make a difference. A high enough proportion of people might once have walked out of those events with their sights newly set. These days, most people are in the audience not to learn anything (it's mostly about slogans anyway) but to direct embarrassing questions to or hurl slander at the representatives of the parties they do not support. These days there is more to be gained in the headline that you did not attend (name recognition means everything) than in spending time to strengthen views that are already deeply rooted. Public debates give each candidate an opportunity to preach to the converted.

A relatively new phenomenon is mass communications through Internet tools like Twitter. Facebook is already losing lustre but is nonetheless still on the list, as is YouTube. These tools are mostly one-way messaging systems that make the sender feel good. The sender believes that he or she is being listened to. It is no longer possible to be a candidate for public office without participating in this kind of one-way communication. I devoted quite a bit of time and energy to getting my perspectives and related images onto Facebook and YouTube, and my team used all of the other Internet tools available. You never know — once in a while, a particular spot goes viral. Getting elected, for novices, is rather like winning a lottery: you have to buy as many tickets as you can.

Of all the traditional activities in elections, including attendance at public events and public debates, door-knocking is the only one still in full favour among party leadership groups and their staff.

The door-knocking you did during your months as candidate-designate before the writ dropped pales in comparison to the kilometres you will be walking over the five weeks of the election. On this round, you will always be surrounded by volunteers, often in the dozens. Whereas before the election was called most residents did not want to be bothered with you, on your rounds during the election you will at least be expected. At a number of doors you may still not be welcomed, but you are unlikely to hear "I didn't know an election was going on!"

Since you will persist in believing that a respectful discourse should allow for at least five minutes of give and take, and since in only one high-rise you might expect to knock on as many as two hundred doors, let's take another look at the math I ran previously. If you use the figures just set out, and if you allow that in a ten-hour day you want to devote three hours to eating and doing other things, it would take about two and a half days to deal honourably with a resident at each door in a medium-sized high-rise. If you have ten such buildings in your riding, this means that before you can turn your attention away from your ten high-rises to the tens of thousands of private homes, the election will already be over.

Door-knocking, as a way to make personal contact with the voters in a riding, is a crock. Politicos and party officials continue to laud door-knocking because it is the quintessential activity that legitimizes the political system in a democracy. But it is a crock. If democracy truly depends upon voters laying eyes on their candidates in person, then democracy has become impossible in most electoral districts across Canada.

And yet, and yet, and yet. Many people will tell you that running for politics is a noble enterprise.

Those people are right.

Those people are right because your run for public office will likely be the only time in your life that you will force yourself to think deeply about the full range of social, economic, and political issues that matter in your riding. Especially during the election itself, but also before, you will be thinking every minute of every day about what might make things better for the people you see on your streets, at their front doors, and sometimes even inside their homes over coffee. For an intense five weeks, you will be subject to a barrage of questions and challenges which tune your mind and ramp up your emotional and intellectual energy because you — especially you the novice candidate — will want to acquit yourself well.

Your fellow candidates, the politicos, will be dragging and bragging themselves through the same processes that you must run through. As I have said, the five-week electoral period is a repeat of the entire gauntlet. At the end, those who ran the gauntlet will feel emotionally beaten and perhaps even a little bit physically hurt. But every single one of the runners, novices and politicos alike, will learn a lot not only about their neighbourhoods and the people who make them up, but also about themselves. At many doors the resident will advise a candidate upon parting, "Try to remember us if you win." Many electors still believe there is a duty owed by a successful candidate in return for their vote.

Because you will be surrounded by core team members and by literally hundreds of volunteers who support you personally or support the party you represent, you will hear each and every hour of every day that you are doing very well. You just might win. Because of your professional background, the odds that your local and regional papers will endorse you as being the best candidate are high. As your support appears to grow and as the endorsements come in, to say nothing of the nods of regard you feel when you see those hundreds of signs with your name emblazoned upon them, your pride will begin to swell. Your determination to not let people down will harden to steel.

In my case, the indicators that I would be staying in this game until I reached the finish line (voting day) grew exponentially in the late winter before what would prove to be an early spring election. I believe I was as ready for this last test of accomplishment as anyone could be.

Marie and I held an important reception at our place on March 21, the first day of spring. Because an election seemed more likely every day, I had spent a great deal of time on the phone and on email to attract as many people as possible. These would again be the people belonging to the 400 Club, the ones I had told I would contact in the days immediately following the dropping of the writ. These would be the people from whom I hoped to solicit up to $10,000 in total contributions within the first week of an election call.

The reception was a wonderful success. We had had to scramble to make it so because a fire on Beechwood Avenue two days before had destroyed the catering business we had contracted with and had burned up the UPS shop which had my printed material ready for pickup. The commitments I received that evening made it possible for me to achieve during the election the contribution total on which I had set my sights. As of March 21, I knew that the basic plan was secure. Almost.

March 21 also happened to be the day the government presented its budget to the House of Commons. The budget was defeated because of the NDP's decision to take a chance in an election. The Liberals had said all along that they would vote against the budget, so there were no surprises there. All three parties had moved themselves so extensively into campaign preparations that, in retrospect, the vote could have gone no other way. For the major parties to turn off their electoral machinery and restart it later would have been more trouble, and more costly, than it was worth. Yet when the writ dropped only a few days after my reception, on March 26, all hell broke loose.

As I have said, I was about as ready as any candidate could possibly be. I had my ducks lined up for the production of all my planned material; Marie had helped to secure offices for our use during the electoral period; Priscilla had returned to Ottawa (from an unexpected and worrisome visit with family in northern Ontario) and had linked us up with an office equipment store to fully outfit the campaign team's office; Priscilla had also already learned what her duties would be and had prepared herself as well as an official agent possibly can; the association had just over $30,000 in its bank account and was primed — after the purchase of signs and front-end payment on our office lease — to turn about $10,000 in cash over to my campaign; we had a basic budget in place that included a direct mailing of our key items to every household in the riding; I had a person, in Luc, who would act as coordinator during the campaign, bring in volunteers, and fill in any holes; we had our list of top supporters who would receive positively requests for more funding; we had a "signs list" of about four hundred confirmed houses where we had permission to display lawn signs; a local merchant had prepared the template for our large arterial signs (the ones alongside city streets and highways) and was ready to produce two hundred of them; we had a list of volunteers ready to start on day one; Marie and I had set up our bank accounts to make a fully transparent loan to the campaign on the day Priscilla called for it; and so on.

Best of all, my campaign plan set down all the steps along the way. We had a "campaign guidelines for dummies" fully written up. The risk of us overspending was close to zero because all members of the campaign team had formally acknowledged that the official agent would not approve any expenses outside of the campaign plan without her or my prior agreement.

Upon my being affirmed as candidate by Elections Canada, we would be in a position to push a few buttons and our planned campaign material would be printed by media outlets and by the UPS store to which we had shifted our flyer and brochure templates. But first, I had to become fully legitimate. I and my campaign and my official agent had to be confirmed as legal by Elections Canada. We needed to have the paperwork signed, sealed, and delivered.

The confirming role of the party leader, however, is the one thing I was not able to control. It is easy to imagine party staffers hovering over the list of intended candidates and having last-minute debates about who stays in and who should be dropped. I was so primed to move forward that I despaired at the thought that the final confirmation of my candidacy might not come through. I was desperately worried about being able to move ahead with everything that I, with the help of a few in the core group, had prepared pre-writ.

As one's confirmation meanders down one side of the mountain from the top, down another side will come directions from party officials. Party officials expect that candidates, through their campaign managers, will do exactly what the party directs. Your party is certain to instruct that all intended communications and planned activities must be cleared in advance by a designated authority. If that dictum gets to your office before you are officially confirmed, given the business ethics you have developed over the years, you just know you will do as you are told. I know I would have. If you don't, and if there is still time to remove you from the official list of candidates, you are almost certain to be dropped.

If I had to set aside all of my prepared advertisements, my flyers, my brochures, the direct mailing of a fun one-page "door-knocker," I would have been setting aside approximately $30,000 of prepared work, including the push-button contracts I had set up which would unleash all of that material, to say nothing of the personal time and the creative efforts of people like Nancy Brown, who had helped me pull the "chair" flyer together. If I had received the direction to buy into party-approved material, I would have been in a financial bind. But I would have done it.

I worried like crazy that the national office of the Conservative Party would get nosy and insist upon blessing the content of all my prepared election material. I worried about this because I had come to understand that elections are big business for the national headquarters of a political party. They are big business for the service providers who have become favourites of the party elite. The national office of all major parties these days do not like candidates acting as independent operators any more than the head office of Harvey's might like a franchisee to feature a menu of special foods.

The CPC national office sent us its list of preferred agents for the production of campaign literature and candidate photographs. Standard templates for brochures and ads were ready to go at National; local campaigns were expected to pay for these and then — at their own added expense — to adjust the templates themselves if they wanted to include a small amount of local content. We in Ottawa–Vanier were not going to be using those agents or any of the national office products. This meant that our campaign would not be contributing to CPC national costs.

Two days into the writ, the prime minister's endorsement came through. (I learned that all CPC candidates, all across the country, were endorsed in a single note from official party leaders to the Chief Electoral Officer. This was the standard approach; I simply had not been told about it.)

Priscilla, now legitimate herself because of the letter I had sent some time ago to Elections Canada and to our official auditor, still held back because she was "waiting for Elections Canada to open their doors." The wait went on and on: each hour seemed like forever to me. She would drive by the Elections Canada headquarters in our riding to check for signs of life and there were none. She did not stop and bang on the door.

While we were waiting, I learned that the national office was at the point of setting up an approvals process: campaign managers would have to submit all material and all activities being planned for their candidate. If we got caught by this initiative, I did not trust that Luc would be able to squeeze us through the process successfully. I needed to launch all of my material before Luc got drawn into National's act.

My growing anxiety put a lot of pressure upon Marie. And Marie was the one who took action.

It was Marie, with Priscilla bound tightly to her side, who went to Elections Canada and banged upon the front doors. The office still looked unoccupied, she told me later, and Priscilla was greatly bothered about making a spectacle of herself. Marie kept banging, to the point where she even worried that the windows might break. And then the door opened.

With Marie glaring at the Elections Canada staff, and with her reminder to one and all that the writ had dropped two days previously, the people in the office did the impossible: I became the first registered candidate in our riding. I was off — up and running. The game, for me, had begun. Priscilla and I were now legal, independent of the association and of the national office.

To my great relief, the order from National to include them in the critical path that delivers products and candidates to market had not yet come. The confirmation of my status as a candidate representing the Conservative Party of Canada came on day two of the campaign, at noon. My paperwork was ready, and before the end of the day, my buttons, consisting of emails and telephone calls, had been pushed. The instruction from party headquarters to clear all material and plans through a newly established coordination office in Ottawa and to use approved templates for campaign literature came on the morning of day three of the campaign.

By then I had already telephoned all my contacts among printers, advertisers, and local and regional newspapers to say "go." The printing had begun, the mailing began, the layout of advertisements was finalized, the dates of delivery of pamphlets and flyers to our office were confirmed, and the furniture had been delivered to our (rather attractive) offices. Sixty thousand copies of my doorknocker were on their way via Canada Post to each residence in our riding and would arrive before the end of the first week. When the order came from the national office that all campaigns needed prior approval for campaign material... the national office was too late.

On the morning of the fourth day, I went down the hill to my office, sat behind my beautiful desk overlooking one of the riding's main streets, and said to Priscilla, "Well, the deed is done! For all intents and purposes, Priscilla, we could go home now and simply await the outcome." My office was not only beautiful, it was also extremely clean and tidy. Priscilla had made it her business, in the evenings of those first few days, to clean the place from top to bottom and to put everything into good order. Wonderful!

I was not entirely serious about having nothing more to do, of course. Just about everything in the electoral process in Canada these days is better understood as a series of discrete events rather than as a process. The events appropriate to electioneering had yet to happen.

Our immediate challenge was to follow up upon our earlier confirmation of where lawn signs could be planted all across the riding. Once our signs were printed and delivered to our storage space in the riding, our task was to hammer posts into the ground and wrap wire around two hundred large signs intended for arterial roadways. I was backed up by a large number of people, including Amy's husband and his father. (The break with my daughters would not happen for another day.) I want to also mention Devon, a man who works on Parliament Hill. He went around with me in inclement weather, teaching me the ropes about sign installation and giving me all kinds of advice in the hours we trudged from location to location in the pouring rain. I had hoped Rob Waters — the "signs guy" in previous Conservative campaigns — would be the lead for all this, but he would be leaving for Florida on day five.

An amusing note came from my son-in-law and his father, who, along an arterial road close to the offices of Mauril Bélanger, decided to exercise our right to plant as many signs as we wanted on public property — adjacent to his front door. Mauril came out personally to complain. When I drove by a few hours later, my signs had all been taken down. In this case, I viewed the actions of the Liberal team to be appropriate, even though we had been within our rights.

I learned that the Liberals would be watching us like hawks throughout the campaign, all across the riding, to pounce upon infractions of Elections Canada regulations attributable to either our sense of fun or our newness at the game. The Liberals had learned to be much more aggressive about campaign-rule violations. All the experience was on their side. Their harping on the rules was one way to destabilize the amateurs in opposition.

The next order of business was the planting of smaller lawn signs in front of the four hundred or so homes where I had received permission through all those calls from the signs list. I learned from Luc after my day spent installing signs along the arterials that Marie and I were the only ones on our campaign team with cars. Our Volvo and our Jeep became service vehicles which delivered signs and staff to all parts of the riding. Since I drove one of the vehicles, I also helped to install most of the signs.

At each door, I stopped to say hello, and thanks. This sometimes delayed things quite a bit.

The preparations we had made for sign delivery and installation paid off: at an early riding event where the prime minister was in attendance, he singled out Ottawa–Vanier as the riding where he saw more lawn signs than anywhere else. He asked me to take a bow on behalf of myself and my team. The material we had prepared in advance was also a success. The "chair" flyer, the size of a large postcard, had been well received. A member of the prime minister's team who lives in our riding had a copy and was waving it about as an example of something really "cool."

My use of our Volvo and Jeep to deliver signs, of course, set a precedent. Throughout the five weeks of the election, our two cars were the only vehicles to take people to neighbourhoods for the walkabouts, the only vehicles to pick up and deliver material, the only transportation available for public events, and so on. I charged for the gas at the end of the campaign, but it took a heck of a toll in personal time. I didn't want anyone else to drive the Volvo!

And now let's look in upon my office arrangements and the supporting cast.

I had picked up two offices down the hill from my home. On the one side was "the candidate's office." On the other was what I called "the train station." The first side was reserved for me and Priscilla. It was available for use by others only on a special-permission basis. I had a key and Priscilla had a key. This office was always very neat, well appointed, very professional. Here is where I met reporters and anyone from the visiting public who wanted to talk to the candidate. Here is where I had private meetings with individual members of the team as required.

On the other side of the hall was "the train station." I called it that because in that office all the hustle and bustle typically associated with a campaign took place. For a few days we lacked adequate communications capacity because our phones and email addresses were still tied to the electoral district association office and no one had thought to leave us the password to gain access. Between Luc and Priscilla, and especially when guided by Marie, new phone lines had to be installed and new email addresses assigned. Luc wanted BlackBerrys for himself and his "senior team," but that had not been included in our basic campaign plan. I believe Priscilla eventually relented. A few hand-held communication devices were added to the mix.

I had appointed Luc to be notionally in charge of what would happen in the train station. I say "notionally" because I had so prepared for the next five weeks that Luc would have precious little to do. All the campaign material was already being produced and mailed. His focus could only be on the "busywork" of campaigning and on the important matter of personnel support.

As the campaign unfolded, I nonetheless grew to be more and more appreciative of what Luc, helped tremendously by Eleanor Brady, was able to achieve in the train station. The national office sent various Parliament Hill staffers our way to help with our campaign as volunteers. Some of these people had had a lot of experience — though few were over twenty-five — and they certainly had energy. Eleanor jumped into her role as volunteers coordinator and fed our new recruits into teams of three and four who walked at least twice daily through our neighbourhoods. We saw right from the start that a couple of fellows (Chris and Geoff) could be trusted to deliver upon the business of door-knocking and polling with remarkable flare and skill. A couple of very effective young women took on the public relations aspects of the work. Marie was on perpetual standby to help resolve tensions between my office and the train station, especially by staying close to Priscilla to help her keep down her temper.

And we had tensions aplenty.

To start with, Priscilla proposed — and I agreed — that the key to my side of the offices (used by Priscilla, and for my formal meetings) not be given to anyone else, not even Luc. Priscilla did not want the calm environment on our side spoiled by the rabble on the other side. Luc — for good reason — found this very upsetting, not least because our office was very attractive and he was planning (I suspect) to use our comfortable furniture and television for personal down time when everyone else went home. Priscilla did not trust Luc and he did not like her.

The dislike between Priscilla and Luc, the two key people on a campaign team, spread into a tension that engaged many other team members. Happily, most of those others could get past the moments of upset and appreciate why my priority always had to be the imperatives of my official agent. We lost only one or two volunteers because of the internecine feuding. I was very impressed to see how the most experienced of our volunteers quickly assessed the situation, took on areas of responsibility at their own initiative, and took charge. I always saw this as a high compliment to me and to the overall effort.

The only occasion we entrusted the key to my office to someone else, by the way, was the early morning Eleanor and a few others went there to watch the Royal Wedding (of William and

Kate) on television. This was toward the end of the campaign when — as luck would have it — a spring storm had knocked out power to large parts of the city but not along the street where our offices were located. (Our home, by the way, was almost burned down because our minds were elsewhere. We forgot to check what some of our candles in the dining room were up to.)

Since most of our money was committed or spent by the end of the first week of the campaign, Priscilla was reluctant to approve any other expenditures. This meant that even taxi money was made available to train-station staff only with great reluctance. Refreshments were funded to a minimal, even laughable amount. Marie and I regularly topped up with our own money what Priscilla provided from the campaign bank account. The amounts were small and could be accommodated within our office allocation for petty cash.

In the campaign's basic plan, we had overlooked basic necessities like garbage cans, soap, toilet paper, and so on for the train station. All of these the train station had to beg Priscilla for.

Marie and I both exploded with laughter (but also tears) when one day Priscilla looked into the train station and muttered, "Pigs!" The place was a mess — an abomination. But those poor guys had none of the usual amenities to keep themselves and their workstations clean. They had no place to stuff piles of campaign literature except one small closet where coats and boots were supposed to be stored.

After the first week, Marie and I decided to sidestep Priscilla's tight controls and began to go down to the offices late at night, every night of the campaign, when everyone else had gone home. We cleaned, we refreshed the water supply, we added chips and comfort foods of various kinds, we provided stamps and letter paper, and so on. When the train-station workers arrived in the mornings thereafter, the place was always in good shape. Since Priscilla rarely deigned to look into their space, she rarely had reason to wonder how the other half managed to keep themselves in such good shape within the very tight allocation of funds that she herself handed over.

Our telephone answering system did not come on stream until after the first week in the campaign; our photocopier and printers regularly broke down (we had three printers by the end of the campaign but were mostly using the ones at the UPS store anyway); arguments among volunteers about favouritism between friends drove some people out and brought new people in.

There were also, though, a great many positive highlights to mark the five weeks of the campaign.

Without regard to the actual order of events, one of these was the national office's agenda for the prime minister. Every time the PM and his wife were in Ottawa during the campaign, there would be a rally. This required the Ottawa-area candidates to show up and be introduced, always to a lot of fanfare. We would run through lines of cheering party supporters (suggestive of the gauntlet?), we would be escorted to private meetings with the prime minister, we might individually be called upon to accompany the PM to a photo-op in our own riding, and so on.

I always welcomed these opportunities to partake in the life of politics, partly because I suspected my time in this life might be short. I even went to the airport reception when the PM returned to Ottawa the day after the election had been won by a Conservative majority. I was the only defeated candidate there and, along with the winning candidates, I received an appreciative hug from the PM.

While on the subject of the PM himself, another highlight of my campaign was having his mother, Margaret, volunteer to do a round of door-knocking with me and my team. Mrs. Harper was a shy, quiet woman who could certainly remind one of her son, the prime minister. Her manner was friendly but somewhat distant. I had her sit in my office for a few minutes, during which I summarized where I thought the campaign in our riding was headed, and then we went to one of the more attractive parts of the riding to knock on doors and drop flyers.

In New Edinburgh, though, Mrs. Harper tripped over a raised flagstone on a walkway. Mrs. Harper appeared to be in her late seventies. Her posture was amazingly straight and this seemed to save the day for us all. She fell forward fully erect. She did not bend a knee. She did not put out an arm. She simply fell full onto the front of her body, landing — it appeared — on every square inch of herself from toe to forehead.

I and one of my team ran to her to help her up and determine the damage, expecting the worst. Yet not a hair, not a piece of skin, not a muscle, not a bone, nothing had been damaged. Not her clothes, not her handbag, not even the flyers that she had been holding in her hand had been disturbed. Once on her feet again, she led the way enthusiastically from door to door as if nothing had ever happened.

I lost the election.

After all the preparatory work, after having been lulled by my own hubris into thinking that I had a good chance to win, I received only a few more votes than Patrick Glémaud had received in the previous federal election, just over 14,000, or 27% of the votes cast. Patrick's campaign had started late, had faltered when his leadership team fell apart within days after the writ dropped, and had required loans from EDAs in Alberta. I had been confident I would do far better than he had done.

As a surprise to me, I came in third, after the NDP candidate.

Readers of this account will notice that in describing the preparations we undertook, I hardly ever mentioned the NDP. The NDP had never done better than a distant third in this riding. I took neither that party nor their candidate seriously. Trevor Hache was an attractive and even tempered young politico who, by his own deportment, clearly had not expected to do as well as he did. The first time I met him, at one of the public events in Vanier, he told me he had not wanted to run again (this was his second time) but the NDP had no one else. His limited background was in social work and community support. From what I could gather, he worked part-time; his major claim to fame, as he repeated often enough during the campaign, was his role in helping to establish a community garden behind the co-op building where he lived.

During the election, though, I could see that the Liberals were beginning to worry about an NDP surge. Whereas most of the questions from other candidates and from the floor had earlier been directed to me, as representative of the party in government, in the last week of the campaign questions began to go to Trevor. I could see that he was confused by this. It was, for the NDP, quite unusual. Worse for him still, the Liberals were wise enough to put their questions in French. Trevor Hache — though his family name is a French one — could not speak the language spoken by a third of Ottawa–Vanier's residents.

The Liberal incumbent received 39% of the vote. This was his lowest ranking ever. He was a few votes under 20,000. Mauril had had reason during the campaign to be nervous. Only three in ten potential voters (because about 40% did not turn up at the polls) would have said "yes" in answer to his pollsters' question: "Will you be voting for Mauril Bélanger in the upcoming election?" Between me and the NDP, we shook him up a bit. The Green Party received about 2% of the votes, less than half their number in the previous election. The big difference for the NDP was a last-week surge of support for that party because of the sudden popularity of Jack Layton.

I suspect that the Liberals, who went down about 5,000 votes from previous numbers, lost most — if not all — of those votes to the NDP. I suspect that my own voting population was essentially the same voting base as is usual for Conservatives in federal elections in our riding. I assess, however, perhaps in self-defence, that Conservative numbers would have been lower if I had not been a good candidate. If the quality of a candidate can explain only 5% of the vote, then I expect my tally would have been about 22% without my effort over my nineteen months in the business.

I am pretty sure that a majority of non-voting residents — most of them new Canadians — would have given their support to the CPC if they had gone to the polls, but, when all is said and done, my guess will never be confirmed. If I had it all to do over again, I would try to attract the government's minister for Immigration Canada (then Jason Kenney) to the riding in the early days of the election. The next federal election, if handled right, could be set up as a test of my hypothesis that attracting a greater number of new Canadians to the voting booths will mean a greater percentage of support for the Conservative candidate.

But for me, that experiment will not happen.

In the months after the May election, I was blown away by the fact that I received not a single message from the national office or the association regarding my future intentions. Except for a nice letter from the prime minister, I got the distinct sense that they were pleased to be rid of me. As Marie observed, the party likely had a grudging admiration for how well the election unfolded, but the emphasis is on the word "grudging" rather than on the word "admiration."

I enjoyed the independence of thought and action that my being the candidate provided. I enjoyed the attention given to me by my supporters, beginning with the prime minister of the country and a number of high-ranking cabinet ministers. I enjoyed the limelight that came along with my being a candidate at public meetings and at private events. For nineteen months, and especially during the election, I was a person with considerable public profile in my corner of Canada's capital city. I enjoyed the prospect of being able to make a difference in my riding.

During the election itself, my profile included signs all over the riding with my name emblazoned upon them. I participated in television interviews and debates where, for the most part, I spoke very well. I was regularly interviewed by regional and local papers, was visited by numerous community leaders who clearly took my candidacy seriously, and was endorsed in the largest regional newspaper, the *Ottawa Citizen,* as being the best — indeed the "ideal" — candidate for Ottawa–Vanier.

On the day of the *Ottawa Citizen* endorsement, just a week prior to the vote, I said to Marie, "This endorsement is what I was running for." I had wanted, once my candidacy began, to have a chance to experience a run for public office and, above even that, to remain credible for as long as I stayed in the game. At the outset, and until the last days of the process, winning the election was not uppermost. The *Citizen* endorsement meant that I had done my job well.

I now believe that the period of the writ is a kind of trauma for those running for public office. Candidates are called upon to be the best they can be, and are almost always on the public stage. After the election there is a degree of post-traumatic stress which reveals itself in dreams and reflections. In my case, running for public office was a totally unexpected development. To then lose in a riding where Conservatives have lost every election since the riding was created could hardly be traumatic in any deep sense of the word. I just wish my luck had been different. I would have loved to surprise everyone — even myself — by concluding my career as a sitting member of the House of Commons.

One of the slogans highlighted in my campaign material was "The courage to act!" After stepping into my role in national-level politics, largely on impulse, I demonstrated the courage to stay the course — and do this honourably — throughout my journey as a candidate. I can be happy about that.

I received a letter from the headquarters of the Conservative Party shortly after the election and, in the margins of this form letter sent to all losing candidates, the president of the party noted, "Rem, you did us proud."

I certainly did! Nothing more needed to be said. I had prevailed through the test of accomplishment.

CHAPTER 9.

LOOKING BACK

Perhaps you are standing at the brink of an undertaking to run the gauntlet. You have just read through the seven tests as I've related them in this book and you're still actively considering running. Remember, the trials and the costs are real. Running for public office at the federal or provincial level in Canada challenges the individual who takes this undertaking on, the people who become part of the candidate's venture, and the political jurisdiction which requires elected representation in its legislatures.

What can a candidate do to prepare for the many tests he or she will have to undergo? What can be done at the federal level to make the competition among party candidates within electoral districts more equal? In this chapter I will give my answer to both these questions.

The tests for a candidate that have been highlighted in this book are those of privacy, values, commitment, leadership, endurance, isolation, and accomplishment. I have likened getting through those tests to running past the whips administered by fellow citizens ranged along both sides of a gauntlet. Sometimes with malice, usually not, the candidate for public office is pressed to show what he or she is made of.

The competition may not be equally hard on everyone running. The novice, for example, is beaten up quite a bit more than the politico because the novice is both unexpected at the starting line and — truth to tell — unwelcome. But all those who emerge at the far end of the gauntlet will have a sense of achievement. They will see in other runners a person who understands, almost a friend. The camaraderie among parliamentarians when Question Period is over happens because, fundamentally, members of Parliament see each other as equals. They see others who, like themselves, had the courage to step into the race, who survived the attempt, and who won.

Being a novice candidate as described in this book, you have an impressive career or working background that will bring gravitas and practical experience from a world outside politics. Your prior association with active politics, however, either was a very long time ago or was passive. How can you know whether you are ready for what is going to happen if you take the next step?

What novice candidates need — what I would have loved to have — is a simple way to rate one's suitability in terms of what lies ahead. Drawing from my experiences, I propose a Readiness Quiz. The questions in the quiz reflect back upon one's career to date while shedding light on what is to come. Potential candidates are likely to plunge in regardless of their test results. The point, however, is not to determine "aye" or "nay." The point is to gird one's loins appropriately, to not be taken by surprise. First-time candidates, whether novices or politicos, should know better than I did what to expect.

The quiz will be interesting not only to novice candidates. I offer it as well to long-time observers of politics in Canada, to professors at universities and colleges, and to their students. I invite to you to add to my ideas the lessons you have learned in the course of wider and more intensive studies. I have merely lived the experience. Others will have the objectivity that has only partially been restored to me by the passage of time.

THE READINESS QUIZ FOR NOVICE CANDIDATES

The Readiness Quiz is presented as a stand-alone document in the appendix to this book. My purpose here is to elaborate on how the sections of the quiz and the questions relate to what has been said to this point. Note, for example, that the seven sections of the quiz pick up the seven tests all candidates must deal with when running the gauntlet. Each question is worded so that a rating of zero means "no" and 10 means a strong "yes."

THE TEST OF PRIVACY (MAXIMUM SCORE: 40 POINTS)

It is assumed that you have no skeletons in your closet. You are not a woman like Claire Underwood — she of *House of Cards* fame — standing for the right to life when she has already had a couple of abortions herself. You are not a person arguing vociferously for getting hard on crime who already has a criminal record. You are not man or woman who is addicted behind closed doors to cocaine. But the more public your life becomes, the more the fifth estate will be looking for real blood to fall onto the ground under your scurrying little feet. If things happened in your life that you'd rather no one ever know about or talk about again, it's best to take a pass. Don't start running.

The questions appropriate for this test are

1. Do members of your immediate and extended family already associate you with the political party that you hope to represent?
2. Do your friends and neighbours already associate you with the political party you hope to represent?
3. Will your personal relationships be enhanced by your standing publicly for the political party you have chosen?
4. Will your professional relationships be enhanced by your standing publicly for the political party you have chosen?

On these questions, my self-rating would have been pretty close to zero. My wife knew what my political leanings were (score 2 points?). Other than that, to everyone else my stepping forward as a full-fledged member of the Conservative Party of Canada was a total surprise (zeros, all around). Even though I had been a contributing member of the Progressive Conservatives and then the Conservatives for over thirty years and had attended a nomination convention or two, I had kept my politics almost entirely to myself. I had personal and professional reasons for this, as well as being an adherent to the admonishment of superior officers in the military: "A gentleman, Mister Westland, does not talk politics with anyone."

On the other hand, if I were to provide the likely ratings for the young man who hopes to replace me as the next CPC candidate for Ottawa–Vanier — a politico who works for a Conservative member of Parliament on the Hill — I would guess 10, 10, 10, and 10. A man or woman from a political family who has long been expected to run for public office and who works on the Hill for a party highly regarded among personal and professional colleagues will be cheered while breezing past this first test of the gauntlet.

The career politician gets 40 out of 40.

If you are a novice, I hope your party affiliation has not been quite so much a secret as mine was. When I said that my own run may have been a folly, I think the test of privacy is the primary reason. Even though I have been a conservative all of my life, it would have been a great deal easier on me to have run for the Liberals, the NDP, or the Greens.

THE TEST OF VALUES (MAXIMUM SCORE: 30 POINTS)

This is a harder test than you might think. It links to the test of privacy and calls upon you to broadcast your personal values.

In the fabled world I laid out in chapter 1, a conservative person will feel a natural bent toward what Conservatives stand for provincially and federally. Liberals will subscribe to liberal values. NDPers will tend toward the social good. The NDP's idea of a social good may even have to be imposed by legislation if too many citizens won't get with the program voluntarily.

When your personal values move onto the public stage to be aligned with political party credos, however, they acquire a sharp edge. You have to know that you are ready for this.

You also have to know that the values ascribed in public to the political party you align yourself with will be ascribed to you, personally, in full. In your personal life you may insist upon a lighter touch. When out in public as your party's representative, however, any attempt to soften before others what a value such as "right to life" means to you personally will be drowned out. Your dithering will be seen as a cop-out or a betrayal.

There are dozens of examples I can offer from my personal experiences on the campaign trail.

Those who know me, for example, can attest that I have never had any problem — none whatsoever — with sexual orientations different from my own. Some of my best memories go back to a time when I found myself in a social circle that included transgender people, transvestites, homosexuals, and others who found comfort among people who lived as they did. My first wife and I were unique as heterosexuals entirely welcome in their company. I remember delightful experiences in the company of one person who, after a career that included time in the military, transitioned from a man to a woman. I stayed on her sailboat off the Florida coast for a week when I needed time to recover from the breakdown of my first marriage.

When I became known as the CPC representative in my riding, I could see doubt enter into my personal relationships with members of the LGBT community. What attitude had really lurked behind my smiling eyes? Was I really as open-minded as I had appeared to be in those long-ago days?

Novices who step forward for one of the other mainstream parties will experience this sharpening of values every bit as much as I did. To support the non-criminalization of abortion, for example, may not be good enough for a Liberal Party which wants its candidates to be strongly pro-abortion. A Liberal with a personal view that is more nuanced may want to keep quiet about it.

There is one particular value, usually listed as a "core" value for us in Canada, that presented me with a particular difficulty: "Do you believe in God?" I described how the electoral district association I was supported by had no doubts. Even before the election was called, during a period when the association's comfort about me engaging with the public was low, a number of members wanted me to spend an hour or two at their respective churches on Sundays to be introduced all around. Before and during the election, I was pressed to stand at the doors of churches, mosques, and synagogues to shake hands with people leaving their respective services and proudly announce my own firm belief in a higher power.

I was happy to go to the church services when invited. I could not agree, however, to trolling the front door of places of worship for votes.

Questions that help you to zero in upon the test of values include the following:

1. Are you comfortable saying what your five core values are to the journalist who interviews you or when you stand on a public stage?
2. Are you comfortable saying which of your core values line up most closely with the values associated with the political party you represent?
3. Will you refrain from saying out loud, when asked, which of the values associated with your party you do not yourself subscribe to?

If I had been asked these questions before I had submitted my name to the CPC electoral district association in Ottawa–Vanier, I would have scored another zero. Once I took hold of myself and realized what I was into, I could have moved myself up toward a rating of 7 or even 8 on the first two questions. On the third of these questions, I would have remained at around a 2, even at the very end. I have a greatly nuanced personal position on the matter of abortion, for example. I learned that trying to deliver myself of it was more trouble than it was worth but I always tried anyway. Those with a strong right-to-life view thought I was betraying the Conservative cause; proponents tending toward the other persuasion thought I was prevaricating, insincere, not to be trusted.

THE TEST OF COMMITMENT (MAXIMUM SCORE: 50 POINTS)

I had no idea at the outset what running for public office would cost me. I had no idea how much I would have to commit in terms of money and people in particular. I was prepared only for the commitment of time. In my diary I record the number of occasions when I took a deep breath and decided — again and then again — to commit my health and my energy. The gauntlets of old were designed to kill you. The gauntlet of an election still can.

By the time you limp out the other end of the gauntlet, if you are competitive by nature and if you have been running for a long time, your commitment will have become total. You will have given all that you have, of every resource available to you. I can hardly believe it even now.

I have already advised that you can make this test easier if — at the outset — you take the time to sit with your spouse or partner, perhaps also with others who rely upon your financial resources (adult children, an aging parent), and let them know what you are about to do. If you already know that you are prepared to commit the time that a successful run for public office will take, you can already say that your revenues from employment will dry up. The longer the run lasts, the more the cupboard will become bare. The financial cost will be in the hundreds of thousands of dollars if you are a novice with a good income that will go unearned for the duration.

No candidate I met got to the other end of the gauntlet without calling upon the services of significant others. I mean by this not only spouses and partners but also adult children, younger kids, babies, parents, grandparents, and long-time friends. The further you get into it, the more likely you are to stumble and need help. You have to hope that those nearest and dearest will help you to lick your wounds — almost always psychological and emotional, thank goodness — in private. Some of those you count upon, unfortunately, may prefer to stand in the rows of the gauntlet and administer a few of the blows.

Here are a few questions to get you started:

1. Have you and your partner agreed that you are able to set aside income-earning opportunities throughout the time of your candidacy?
2. When the writ drops, you will be inundated with volunteers, but not before. Are you able to count upon at least ten family members or close friends to provide the help you will need, when you need it, between the time you are nominated to the time that the writ drops?
3. Do you have experience asking for money from family and friends?
4. Are you comfortable with asking associates and strangers for money, in increments of $200 to $1,500?
5. Do you have a track record of bringing associates and strangers together in a pursuit that, in the end, will benefit you — if you are successful — to a far greater extent than it will any of them?

My overall score, yet again, would have been low.

The novice who comes into politics from a business or a profession that includes money-raising and team-building as regular activities will be greatly helped at this point in the race. Politicos are likely to be people already working inside of, or in direct support to, the political party of their choice. They will have spent many weeks on the campaign trail in support of party candidates, often beginning this activity when still children. Family support and raising money are about as familiar to the politico as breathing and eating. If a politico scores less than 40 on these questions, it will be a young person who is just getting started.

THE TEST OF LEADERSHIP (MAXIMUM SCORE: 20 POINTS)

Here is where the novice might expect to shine. But the problem is that leadership is not a highly valued commodity among party candidates these days. Even at the cabinet level when a political party is in government, we have seen how a cabinet minister who speaks his or her mind on a subject can expect to be relegated to the backbenches.

The test of leadership becomes a test of your ability to be a good follower, one whose capacities have been proven in your previous fields of endeavour but who is comfortable setting those capacities aside in order to do what the "boys in short pants" tell you to do. A retired military general running for the Liberals, for example, has value because having a general in the ranks may bring credit to the party. That person's leadership skills risk screwing things up mightily, however, if those skills are exercised among people who are determined to run a contemporary campaign based upon image and numbers.

I believe there is more to politics than winning elections. Candidates, in their person, are challenged to bring credit and honour to the political system. Elections are not possible without candidates, and elections are degraded by candidates who allow themselves or the people they hope to represent to be made light of. The longer you, the novice, are a candidate, the more you will have to step out in front of a process that is interested in data and make of it a process that is fundamentally about people. You have seen how, in my case, my taking charge became essential. My personal reputation depended upon it. I think I made a greater contribution by emerging from the gauntlet with my honour intact than I would have done had I submitted myself to the science of politics.

When leadership is not a valued commodity, the formulation of questions becomes a bit of a challenge. One is looking to place a numerical value on positives but also on negatives. Here, however, are questions for this test:

1. Would you say that you are widely known in your riding for your ability to command and to lead?
2. Are you prepared to give yourself over to the leadership of others even if your reputation for leadership has become at stake?

Being widely known for strong and effective leadership in your riding merits the maximum of 10. Recognition of this kind will advance you in your effort to obtain "name recognition" among voters, and your party will appreciate this. A score of less than a 10 on the second question, however, advertises to your electoral district association that you might become a problem.

A young politico, one with a background of leadership in high school or university, might rate himself or herself a 5 on question one and a 10 on question two. An older politico, by now a career politician, would score 10 on both.

In my case, I would have scored myself at a 6 on question one. In my public material I could certainly make a pitch for proven leadership, on issues of direct interest to the riding to boot, but I had not operated at a level that had made me well known outside my professional circles. On question two my self-rating would have been zero. On this test I would have achieved a combined total of 6.

Overall, I am not doing so well so far, am I?

THE TEST OF ENDURANCE (MAXIMUM SCORE: 40)

A candidate who is designated months before being confirmed when the writ drops will know how tough this test can be. Between designation and confirmation, all the other tests may serve no higher purpose. You can be dismissed at any time.

This test is much more demanding upon the candidate who takes the period between elections seriously. Designated candidates have the option to just sit back and watch, or to become active only when prepared and prodded by others. In their past lives, novices will often have seen the colleague or associate who basically rides the surf, stays out of trouble, and gears up for action only when it's closing time. In your run for public office you will see incumbents who are stirred to life in your riding only in the last month or two before the writ drops. In Ottawa–Vanier, during the election, the Liberal incumbent pumped his fists, wore a bright red scarf, and promised to lose one pound of weight for every two days of the campaign. Image, not substance, was his purpose.

Political parties of all stripes have learned that it is safer to designate a future candidate as close to the time of an election as possible. The test of endurance puts not only the candidate at risk: it puts the party at risk as well.

If a tired or unhappy candidate slips up badly on the test of privacy and inappropriate words slip out, for example, the party has to go on the defensive immediately. If the test of commitment demonstrates that a novice candidate, selected for his or her deep pockets, has no interest in making top-level donations to the party or even to his or her own campaign preparations, the electoral district association may press headquarters to anoint a replacement.

In my case, the test of endurance saw me get close to the edge a number of times. In the depth of many lows, I would be poised to jump off on my own steam or positioned to be pushed off by those around me. I was unable to accept the desultory approach of my association so I grabbed more and more initiative away from them and thereby put my candidacy at risk. I recall one almost amusing exchange four months into my candidacy. The president of my electoral district association ordered me to do as she instructed or she would get me kicked out. I remained recalcitrant. She was so angry, she picked up her notes and prepared to walk straight out of the apartment we were in, but her husband held her back. The apartment we were in was her own.

The following statements address the test of endurance. Assign a zero if you do not agree at all and a 10 if you strongly agree.

1. Rites of passage in social or professional settings are a useful way to demonstrate character and prove aptitude.
2. The highs of a personal or professional experience are almost always worth the lows.
3. Quitting a pursuit, once you have committed yourself to it, is never an option.
4. Completing a task in which others around you have a stake and a profound interest can be more important than health itself.

I would have done well on these four questions. Rites of passage at military college were more than soft torture — they led us to prove something to ourselves, in the recruit class, and to senior cadets. I would score myself a 10 on question one. I would then rate questions two through four at 8, 6, and 9.

Had my party used a measurement tool equivalent to my Readiness Quiz, I suspect I would have been dropped as a potential candidate before my examiners moved from the test of privacy to the test of values. Had I stayed on the list until my answers to the test of endurance were rated, however, I would have been able to recover some lost ground.

THE TEST OF ISOLATION (MAXIMUM SCORE: 30)

This is not a pleasant test to elaborate on. What it comes down to is whether you are okay with the personal cost of transitioning from a private to a public person, meaning the strong likelihood that people, places, and things that mattered to you in your private life have to be parked or discarded in order to be effective in a public space. The importance and strength of your relationship to others will change.

Most people who aspire to responsible opportunities in public life as elected representatives will loudly declare that the trade-offs and the discarding do not have to be made. Most people will say the same thing about ascendency of any kind, including within their places of work.

To become an executive director in your company, you might say, did not mean that you and your partner stopped socializing with the baggage handlers and tradespeople you shared your lives closely with during the ten years of your rise to this new position. To be promoted to colonel in the military did not mean that you stopped hanging out with the majors and captains you went camping with and drank with at the mess. To become a star in the acting profession in Toronto did not mean you had to hire a new set of agents, move to New York or Hollywood, and acquire a new husband or wife.

But of course success in any venture means all of those things. The political theorist Thomas Hobbes, in his 1651 book *Leviathan*, provides an eloquent argument in regard to the fundamental equality in talent among all people.

The force that drives one of us to the top and another over sideways is opportunity, on the one hand, and networking on the other. Most successful people are highly networked with others whom they vainly perceive — paraphrasing Hobbes — to be equally as wise as themselves.

One of the first things I was told when joining up with the Ottawa–Vanier electoral district association was that I would not win the nomination convention because I had no network. After I became the candidate I was exhorted to network like crazy. Most candidates who become members of Parliament must change their networks again and again, as must most successful people.

The questions that capture the severity of this test, therefore, are the following:

1. In your record of achievement to date, have you had to

change your network of professional associates along the way?
2. In your record of achievement to date, have you had to change your network of friends along the way?
3. How strong is the interest of your family and friends in being a part of your future in politics?

I believe most novices, if they are honest, will score almost as high on these three questions as would politicos. Most novices traded up from shop-floor friends to executive-level colleagues as their careers progressed. For politicos, politics and its network of activists has been life itself. My situation was special, to my own disadvantage, because the truth is that all my life I have eschewed networks. To describe in detail why I believe what I say about myself to be true, however, might suggest an uncertainty on the matter that I do not feel. My rating for myself would be zero on questions one and two, perhaps a score of 2 on question number three. My wife would have been standing by my side during a round or two in elected office, but rarely with a smile on her face.

THE TEST OF ACCOMPLISHMENT (MAXIMUM SCORE: 30)

Accomplishment, or completion, to add yet another word to the inventory of words I could have loaded onto this test, harkens to a person's determination to succeed, to follow through, to finish well, to still be there at closing time. This is the only test that, if failed, will be of no consequence for a person's clearance to run for public office. The test is applied only after the writ has dropped and the designated candidate has been officially confirmed by the party leader and has been made a legal entity — together with the official agent and official auditor — for the duration of the writ.

To my mind, this test is rather like a mirror. You get to look at yourself, at all that you have done to get this far, and the question is whether you will drive your project home in the ways that you had planned.

At this point your electoral district association no longer holds sway over you at all. The association has ceased to function. It can no longer raise or spend money. Your own campaign team holds the reins. You and your official agent hold *all* the reins. Your party can make things difficult for you if you are uncooperative but you would not have gotten this far if that had all along been somewhere in your character or your intent. The gauntlet would have beaten your negative proclivities into the open. Your party will know by now who and what they have on their hands.

The significance of this test, this look into the mirror, is what it says about the kind of elected representative you will become if you are elected. The most intense round of your candidacy begins when the writ drops. Everything moves so very fast.

Dozens of new people will come on board to advance the cause of your party in your riding. They will be expecting to carry you on their shoulders, with you shouting slogans haphazardly into the air while they run you from place to place. Your party will unload a portfolio of election material at the doorstep of your campaign office and invite you — nay, instruct you — to choose your favourites from among the flyers, leaflets, and pamphlets that you see in there.

Now is the time to confirm whether you will remain your own person. Do you intend to stay on the track that you have laid down for yourself? Finishing the race is now almost inevitable. You will literally have to die in order to put a stop to the election in your riding.

How well you finish will still matter to you personally, but you should know that the leaderships of today's political parties care very little about their candidates' proven capacities with regard to this test. For them the only matter of consequence is whether you add a seat to the total required in the House of Commons to form a majority government (in the best outcome) or to be the official opposition.

In the Quebec riding of Berthier–Maskinongé in 2011, the NDP fielded a candidate who knew nothing about the riding at all and who did no campaigning whatsoever. Yet she won. Hers was one of the most stunning displays of candidates being a cipher and a placeholder. For her party, as will be the case soon for all the others if my predictions bear out, success was all about central messaging and party leader profile. The young lady, I am told, remains extremely proud of her party's achievement in a riding to which she was a total stranger. Her party was not in the least embarrassed. She intends to run again.

The questions I propose for this test are

1. Do you agree with the military college slogan "Anything that is worth doing is worth doing well"?
2. When projects you initiated in your professional life were completed, was it important for you to be on hand to close the deals?
3. In the last mile of a marathon, should the runner stick to the game plan?

My ratings on questions one, two, and three would be 10, 8, and 9.

I am pretty sure the CPC knew I would be taking my campaign to the finish line on the basis of principles and material that I had prepared well beforehand. I was running in a riding that would not have been on any of their screens at party headquarters anyway, so they could take a chance and give me a pass. They knew by then that I would not embarrass the party because I most definitely would not be embarrassing myself.

The ways in which political parties use a quiz such as this, should a candidate make his or her test results known, would say a lot about how those parties perceive the significance of the electoral process in Canada. To score high on the first half of the quiz is to advertise one's adaptability to life as a politico. I suspect political parties would, each and every one, disqualify aspirants with ratings as low as mine would have been.

My primary purpose with this quiz, however, is to help novices assess their personal aptitude to take on the challenges that candidacy for public office entail. The Readiness Quiz is my answer to this question: "What can be done to help novice candidates be better prepared?"

And now, with regard to the second of the two questions I asked at the beginning of this chapter, let's consider what could possibly be done to make the competition between novices and politicos in the electoral process more equal.

I have no intention of wrestling for myself a spot among the columnists, pundits, academics, agencies, and associations already vying for public attention to their ideas for electoral reform. My purpose, drawing entirely from one person's experience, is to put on the table something else for those experts and those dedicated bodies to take into account. There may be cause for them, in their own individual and collective thinking, to make some adjustments to what is already being said and written. I am too far along in my private life to compete for airtime.

I will begin my shift toward conclusions and recommendations with some strong and positive words. I am not a poet, but I want to use an unusual structure of partial sentences to get the emphasis right:

In order for democracies to work effectively,

it is of profound importance

that the men and women who vote upon legislation which impacts their fellow citizens

be people who regularly and personally

experience the travails of a fair electoral process.

The disinclination of "good people" to spend the time, money, and personal capital (family, friends, professional colleagues) to engage in the electoral process as novice candidates is unlikely to change. The welcome of novice candidates among the politicos is unlikely to increase. But the gauntlet of expectations, hopes, and demands that a candidate must run through during the period of an election will always be a wake-up call for every candidate — novice or politico, young or old. For politicos, elections will always include the risk of electoral upset because of how political winds may blow. The gauntlet that must be run includes slights and insults. It includes onerous trials which engage friends and family. The candidate, whether a novice or a long-time (even if still very young) politico, will always emerge at the other end somewhat chastened. Somewhat humbled. Somewhat ennobled by the intensity of the effort.

The personal tests that an election imposes are meaningful. This is true notwithstanding that the citizens who line up along both sides of the gauntlet represent only a small percentage of the number who will vote.

The more populous our ridings become in the future, the fewer will be the chances for a resident to discuss political issues with a candidate. In future years residents will vote for a "favoured" candidate knowing even less than today about who that candidate is. The vote for a local candidate will increasingly be a response to what is communicated from party headquarters. That communication will be in slogans and vague promises that have little meaning on the ground. The difference a candidate can make to his or her own chances are today held to explain under 5% of the overall result. That percentage will go down in future years, not up. From a numbers perspective, when it comes to whether a political party wins or loses, the characteristics of individual candidates will become redundant.

I think this growing redundancy is regrettable and should be resisted. But a democracy which features a large cohort of politicos is not necessarily a lost cause. Would Canada's foreign policy in recent times have fared better under a clone of Lester Pearson than it did under the lifelong politicos Joe Clark or John Baird? Were the Canadian Forces better managed by former general Gordon O'Connor than by the lifelong politico Peter MacKay? I think the record shows that politicos are just about as trainable once elected to Parliament as are the novices who came into electoral politics with a well-rounded background. Politicos may even be preferable to star candidates who, having achieved all they can in their business or professional careers, hope to use the powers of the state to further personal goals.

Taking steps to ensure that a few dozen novices are likely to make it into the House of Commons in each election, however, will give hope to those of us who want to see more sophistication in the place. Hannah Arendt, the philosopher who became famous for the phrase "the banality of evil" (*Eichmann in Jerusalem*, 1963) might have me add that the capacity to think independently may one day be essential for our individual and collective well-being. Novices, by my description, are not joiners. When the chips are down, they will dare to stand apart and continue speaking for the humanity in us all.

What bothers me much more is pretence. Elections in Canada feature all kinds of activities and busywork that provide flak cover for the deterioration of representative democracy. If we want to make things better, it is important to build upon a realistic appreciation of how things really are. There was a joke going around when I was a kid which will help me make my point.

There is this guy, see, who stands on a corner of two busy streets in Toronto. He is energetically flapping his hands. His hands are limp at the wrists, so the impression he makes is quite a foolish one. When asked what he is doing, his answer is "I am keeping the elephants away." The return, of course, is "There are no elephants around here." The rejoinder from the fool, as a look of achievement spreads on his face, is "You see? It's working!"

In the electoral process in Canada's democratic system, a whole lot of hand-flapping is going on. Hands are flapped during every election to ensure that the image of Canada's democracy stays vibrant and strong even while democracy itself may be failing. Because Canada's governments at every level continue to be among the most successful in the world, it seems to almost everyone that the flapping of hands is working.

Superfluous efforts, perhaps once very meaningful, now dramatize a myth. Those efforts draw an audience into a delusion of democracy in action. To see candidates running from door to door and place to place — literally running, with supporters holding papers and satchels chasing behind — is to see hands flapping. Candidates, especially winning candidates, will affirm at the end of an election that they met personally with thousands of residents. At best they will have met with 10% of the voting public. Their boasts are akin to the useless flapping of the fool's hands.

To see candidates nod and grimace at residents who open their doors for a three-second verbal salute and then to hear candidates say that they have gauged the attitudes of the voting public through discussion and listening is to see hands flapping. If a meaningful exchange takes at least ten minutes, the great likelihood is that the percentage of the voting public for whom an oral exchange was meaningful is extremely low.

To see candidates throw literature onto the doorsteps of businesses and private homes and then to hear their campaign teams say that they have spread the word on what their candidates stand for is to see hands flapping. The content of that literature is mostly bumph, a lockstep uptake of exactly the same messages as are being bombarded upon the public through media of all kinds by each political party's central headquarters. The uptake of the material by residents appears to be 99%, but this is because most people do not like to leave garbage on their doorsteps. Almost no one reads the contents as they carry the stuff to their recycling bins.

To see candidates participate in debate with other candidates on public stages or on television and the Internet is to see hands flapping. It is rare to draw more than 100 people to a public debate. In most ridings you need around 20,000 votes to win. It is rare to hear that the audience watching the broadcasts is more than a couple of thousand. You need around 20,000 votes to win.

To spend a whole lot of campaign money during an election to build up data on who your party's supporters are and to say that this exercise will help you to win the election is to flap your hands like the fool. You need 20,000 votes to win. To make telephone calls or seek return information via email in a riding of 60,000 voters takes much more time and resources (both people and money) than can be raised and expended during the five weeks of a campaign. In practice, it amounts to busywork. It can — at best — result in improved data on 5,000 or so voters. Those data will not be reliable by the time of the next election. Very little, if anything, will be done between elections to keep those data up to date. If, in a riding such as mine, our data had been stunningly accurate and our demon diallers had helped to ensure that all 14,000 Conservative Party supporters got out to the polls, I would have known for certain that I would lose. We would have annoyed everyone else, and I needed 20,000 votes to win.

To devote a team of supporters, cars, pizzas, and beers to a strong "get out the vote" (GOTV) drive on election day is to flap your hands wildly about. At best you will be able to ferry a few hundred people to the polls. Half of these will be supporters of competing parties who are pleased to accept the services you have provided for free.

It is amusing, but really kind of sad, to watch political parties, political scientists, pundits, columnists, elections agencies, and even courts get wrapped around the axle over tangential issues like robo-calls. It is amusing because those irritating telephone calls by cynical campaign team members will influence such a small percentage of the vote. It is sad because, by focusing upon unethical practices that affect the vote in ones and the twos, the people and the institutions who should be worried about the state of democracy in Canada are allowing the fundamentals to fall apart without comment.

As the hands flap during our elections the crowds gather around the foolish candidates and ask what they can do to help. Everyone is satisfied that the elephants are being kept at bay. We are all very certain there will never be the need for an "Arab Spring" in Canada.

I want to take a poke at those in the crowd who dance around the fool with the flapping hands and cry, "What we need is proportional representation!" In my view the only meaningful impact of the hand-flapping — and it is of profound importance — is upon the bodies, minds, and spirits of the candidates themselves. Those hands are like the sticks that were once wielded when gauntlets had to be run by miscreants who were undergoing punishment or by youth who were being tested.

To change Canada's "first past the post" elections approach to one where a significant number of aspirants for public office no longer have to run the gauntlet would not only reinforce the power of the centre. It would create a system where the one piece that still ennobles participants in the process is removed. Proportional representation, where it means that people high enough on a party's list do not have to run at all, would be wrong. In my view all those who ultimately sit in places where laws and regulations are voted upon must have had the courage to run the gauntlet which has public office waiting on the other end for the few who win.

Would-be dictators and tyrants who have won office in failed or failing democracies act quickly after their elections to ensure they never have to run the gauntlet again. There is a kind of "hunger games" echo in an electoral approach (proportional representation) if the variant being championed is one which allows a small number of party elite to watch party representatives run electoral races in order to build up the points which will bring the elites themselves into power. If it proves ultimately impossible to hold back the growing momentum in favour of proportional representation (all party elites will jump onto this bandwagon one day), my recommendation is that a person cannot stay on the preferred list of a political party unless that person has personally run somewhere and has obtained at least 20% of the vote in the political jurisdiction where he or she ran.

The public at large, while perhaps disdainful of the political system overall and of politicians in particular, have an intuitive awareness that the people who end up in the House of Commons (federal) or legislative assemblies (provincial) have sacrificed something in order to get there. The candidates who lost sacrificed every bit as much and often — in the case of novices — much more. I think it is important from time to time to remind people of this. Perhaps there should be a medal of some kind that can be publicly worn by every candidate who was credible enough to draw 10% or more of the vote.

Citizens in a democracy are more likely to respect the authority of democratic institutions and leaders if they know that somewhere in the process the electorate — even if in relatively small numbers — can impose upon their leaders the eating of humble pie. This includes the stress that EDAs can impose upon their candidates. Members of those electoral district associations, notwithstanding what I have said about their competencies, insist upon the privileges that come with membership. Chief among these is to be first in line, their whips at the ready, when the run of eager aspirants for public office begins, during the nomination process. All other citizens get the chance to ask questions and demand better of their aspiring leaders when the writ drops.

At the association level, candidates are personally known by those whose vote they seek. The political record in Canada is replete with examples of candidates, including sitting members of Parliament or of provincial assemblies, who have upset their association and have paid a price for that. The veto right of party leaders, almost always the target of political pundits and commentators, has certainly compromised the intended role of EDAs. But if an EDA's preferred candidate is not endorsed, you can bet that the party's preferred alternative candidate will have an even tougher run than usual. The whips held by EDA members cut more deeply than those in the hands of other riding residents.

Running for public office is too hectic an activity to enhance a person's understanding of political theory. I came into this activity with a background in political theory. I am not much wiser about the democratic process now than I was before. My heavy dose of practice, however, prompts a few practical considerations.

First, I have observed that the sitting member of Parliament or of a legislative assembly is like a professional competing against amateurs. This can be changed between elections by spreading the money now provided to sitting members around to the EDAs of all registered parties in a riding.

I have learned that the public funds now regularly doled out at the federal level to the offices of sitting MPs were intended, back in the Trudeau years, to help members of Parliament equip themselves on the Hill to delve fully into the omnibus bills that the Trudeau government introduced to Parliament. Some MPs used the money in the way intended. The minister for whom I was executive assistant, for example, hired a senior advisor to pore through cabinet documents and government program proposals to give our minister some independence of thought in the government's decision-making process. Most MPs, however, and now likely all of them, instead used the money to strengthen their hand locally, for the next election. Most MPs remain too weak on the Hill to do a competent job reviewing omnibus bills, but they are stronger than ever on the ground.

Second, a person elected to public office could be limited by convention or legislation to a maximum of two successful elections, or eight consecutive years, in public office representing the same riding. Being a member of Parliament, remember, is not a job. It is a series of functions. It is not so complicated that the work improves after ten years of experience. Indeed, the NDP say they are very pleased with the performance of their surprise candidates. The candidates who hold their chairs indefinitely become enchanted by their own entitlements, rather as if those entitlements were a royal prerogative.

Fixed terms would mean that successful politicos would have a harder time whipping already weak EDAs into submission. Sitting politicians would have to worry about finding jobs outside of the realm of politics, and pension costs will go down. There would be new faces in electoral competitions on a fairly regular basis, and EDAs — the bulwark of electoral participation in Canada because of how they can link riding residents to candidates — would become more influential.

If an elected politician is particularly effective (a party leader, premier, prime minister), the alternative to that person stepping away from office would be to find another riding after eight consecutive years. People whom political parties want to keep in public office should be good not only for the party but also for more than one riding in the country.

I had contemplated, as an alternative to imposing a maximum term limits, the idea of shutting down MP pensions. The Liberals, under Prime Minister Louis St. Laurent, introduced pensions to the House of Commons back in 1952, perhaps to pump up the advantage of incumbency (the Liberals were headed toward a future as "the government party of Canada") while also compensating MPs who no longer had the time to run back home to save ongoing business interests. Pensions should stay, but it should be harder to earn them.

Third, I believe the power of party leaders to veto an EDA's proposed candidate should be limited to the week immediately after the association has made its proposal. The EDA should still have the option to change its mind, but now the party leadership should get involved. EDAs are currently not very strong. EDAs can be extremely fickle owing to internecine feuds. Party leaders should not bow too easily to an EDA's demand that a candidate it once recommended should later be removed.

My mind's eye with these recommendations is upon the thesis put forward by the political theorist John Rawls, in his book *A Theory of Justice* (1971). The electoral system, embracing EDAs, their candidates, and the citizens in each riding, should be designed so that someone standing behind a "veil of ignorance" — someone who does not know where he or she will land in the world — believes that the chances for success are reasonably equal no matter where the landing happens.

So there you have it.

You should not expect sweeping changes from a conservative. We conservatives are tinkerers. There is, nonetheless, one change, perhaps radical in contemporary times, that I would absolutely make if I had the power. I would make it an offence for any organization to gather data about the voting intentions of Canadian citizens. If the worst happens and our democracy becomes so weak on the ground and so centralized in our governing capitals that concentrating forces in our economy are able to take over at the political helm, I would hate to have armed those leaders of tomorrow with data that confirm who are their friends and who their enemies.

CONCLUSION

When the governor general of Canada, on the advice of the leader of the government, issues the writ which orders the next federal election, will the approximately 1,300 Canadian citizens running for the 338 available seats in the House of Commons be running for the people?

The short answer is "no." Almost all of those who win nominations and become designated candidates for upcoming federal or provincial elections will be running for the political party they represent. There will still be two or three hundred "novices," people with extensive backgrounds outside of politics who are new to the game and whose purpose is both greater than themselves and broader than the ideology of the party they stand for. There will be a few dozen "independents," people who have no party affiliation. Whether the independents are running for vanity, out of pique after being dropped from party lists, or for a thrill does not matter: they will almost certainly lose.

The vast majority of candidates will be young or aging politicos, men and women who committed themselves unreservedly to the party they are running for when they were just starting out in life. For many, as in the case of the one aging politico and two young activists I ran against, the commitment to their respective parties began in high school or university and has not wavered since.

Does this matter? Does it matter that political parties today, if they were to administer the quiz attached as an appendix to this book, would prefer to take on those who score the very highest? Does it matter that universities and colleges, along with specialized institutions like the Manning Institute, are training young people how to be candidates for public office as if winning an election is tantamount to the start of a long career?

I think it does matter.

There is a crucial difference between candidates who mean to take the views of their electorate into the heart of political parties, on the one hand, and candidates who have been chosen or trained to deliver party lines to the electorate, on the other. To go, on a large scale, from one type of candidate to the other is to turn democracy on its head.

Political parties for whom candidates are conveyors and apologists for centrally inspired messages and policies become tools of the central elite that run them. Ian Kershaw's account of German politics in the first half of the twentieth century elaborates on what can happen when political parties use their members as tools to wield party power.

These days to even ask the question "Are you running for the people?" is to display a naivety that merits a deep red blush. How could I have thought that my run was about anything other than the policies and politics of the Conservative Party of Canada? Why did I think that my having been executive assistant to a federal government minister in the seventies and early eighties might make a difference? How could my subsequent thirty years as a senior executive in the public and private sectors make my candidacy any more attractive to the voters in Ottawa–Vanier?

Four years after the event, I can acknowledge that I was indeed naive. When a few (very few) residents received me at their doors with the words "Thanks for doing this," I believed at the time that they were thanking me on behalf of the electorate as a whole. They were thanking me, I thought, for offering up my proven competencies. I believed they were acknowledging that I, if elected to the House of Commons, would have the maturity and perspective needed to talk back to party leaders and to evaluate the advice provided by career public servants. I now suspect that those few were committed Conservative Party supporters. They were thanking me for representing the party they would have voted for regardless.

Soon after my candidacy was announced in a popular local newspaper, one of my neighbours asked, "I suppose you were unable to find anyone else to do it?" In my naivety, truth to tell, I was taken aback by that comment. I had expected polite recognition of the personal costs I was taking on. In the euphoria of my having taken up a challenge that I believed to be important in a democratic society, I had expected my neighbour to congratulate me and wish me luck. I now know what she meant. People with extensive backgrounds like mine who nonetheless fall short of the designation "star candidate" have become a rarity. She was as much taken aback by the surprise of my candidacy as I was by her comment on the matter.

Most Canadians have become comfortable with a drift away from an age when candidates for public office stood for something in their own right, separate from the political party they chose to represent. Today the majority of first-time and repeat candidates have been partisan for a very long time, even if they are still under thirty. They are extremely proud to be aligned with anything and everything that their party is known for. A newly elected member of Parliament who answered, when asked how she got into politics, "I always loved the NDP" is now the norm. She was not running for the people — how could she have been? She did not know any of the people in the riding she was elected to represent. She did not even speak their language.

First-time MPs who knuckle down and do their jobs — meaning that they expend the public funds and have the energy needed to implement the functions of public office — have a better than even chance of winning a second time, and a third, and becoming career politicians. If they acquire profile within the permitted bounds of their party's ideology, the career politicians can become competent stewards of the public interest, at least as defined by their party. They can become ministers of federal and provincial cabinets. They can become prime ministers and premiers. But the base on which their governments' decisions are made will become increasingly narrow.

"Our political class is now dominated by career politicians," writes Donald Savoie, Canada Research Chair in Public Administration and Governance at the University of Moncton, in an October 2014 article in *The Globe and Mail*. "They start younger and rise to the top a lot faster." He then comments upon the backgrounds of three of the last four premiers in his province and makes a point that applies equally well to many of the career politicians who assume cabinet-level positions federally: few had gained any meaningful experience in other sectors before ascending to the top jobs in the government of this country. His observations throughout that article, inspired by what he has seen over years of personal interaction with senior leaders in Canada's administrative and political structures, resonate well with what I have observed of the electoral process.

My nineteen months in the trenches of participatory politics led me toward the set of questions that explains how elections in Canada have come to favour the career politician. It is very simple, really. It begins with self-selection. The young and older politicos who become career politicians score significantly higher on those questions than do the first-time novices. It is much easier for the politico to run through the gauntlet of tests imposed upon all candidates in the electoral process. Because it is so much easier, the politico is much more likely to say "yes" when the opportunity to run presents itself. Most first-time politicos have been looking for the chance to run long before it came their way.

For politicos, the first obstacle in the test of privacy, the need for a person contemplating candidacy to publicly confess his or her political orientation, is hardly a test at all. For them, it has long been a matter of pride to crow about their party affiliation from the treetops. For the politico the public values of the party have become personal values. The second test, the test of values, is a no-brainer as well.

Most politicos start young. The test of commitment, for them, is another fly-by. For the middle-aged novice, however, for whom the tests of privacy and values were already gruesome enough, there is a large mortgage and kids in university. Family and friends of the older novice are themselves quite far along life's continuum of experience and age. Health is likely not a factor for the first-time politico or for his or her coterie of enthusiastic supporters.

The test of leadership is another demoralizer for the novice who is greatly experienced. To learn that one's talent for leadership and one's management skills are not wanted by an association that is severely lacking in both, or by the "boys in short pants" who descend from party headquarters from time to time to tell you what to do, is greatly aggravating in a context where losing one's temper is not an option.

And what about the test of isolation? The politico has learned how to bond very quickly with those who can help an aspiring career politician speed toward his or her goal. The novice slowly and painfully learns that private relationships pull away as one's persona becomes more public. The politico is eager to meet the next rainmaker who will gather supporters and raise funds on his or her behalf. The novice ends up doing much of this alone, because there is no established network for someone who comes from away.

How do Canadian elections favour politicos or, as Savoie calls them, career politicians? The answer, once again, is: by making it far easier for them to run through the gauntlet of personal tests in an election than it is for novices.

Most Canadians who have learned a thing or two outside of politics are smart enough to know that the odds against a novice in the electoral process are very long. They know intuitively that it is an unfair competition. The thirty-year-old with a narrow background, whose knowledge is often limited to the arcane business of advising elected representatives in federal or provincial legislatures, will get to the other end of the gauntlet unscathed. He or she is also much more likely to win.

Most Canadians with a background comparable to my own, in other words, are smart enough not to do what I did. When an opportunity to run for public office drops unexpectedly into their laps, they decline. And when they decline, they share their reasons with family, friends, and neighbours. The news spreads that running for politics and — by extension — being a politician is not something that people of proven competence in anything other than politics itself should consider.

In the previous chapter, I suggested a number of ways in which competition for elected office at the federal and provincial levels can be made more equal.

Something can also be done to reinforce the opportunity of interested Canadians to poke and prod those who stand for the political parties during an election. The more political parties become centralized, the more important it will be to get an adequate measure of the elected representatives through whom party powers are delivered. Those people will ultimately be our best defence against democracy being hijacked by self-serving party elites.

The gauntlet requires each and every candidate, party leaders and backbenchers alike, to run the risk that he or she may be exposed in some way that undermines his or her chances for victory and — more significantly — the chances of their party securing one more number toward the coveted majority of seats in the legislature.

To this point in the conclusion I have said nothing about the tests of endurance and accomplishment. These two tests can be manipulated to increase the opportunity for an interested electorate, and certainly for mainstream and Internet media, to confirm that those running for election are as suitable for public office as they purport to be.

Because of the risk that comes with exposure during the intensity of an election, governing parties typically hold the period of the writ to the five-week minimum. Candidates are often selected only weeks or days before the writ drops. When candidates are designated months prior to an election, I learned, electoral district associations try to keep them under wraps. Designated candidates are kept busy with the "science" of politics. They are reminded that "designation" as candidate will not be the same as formal appointment until the day after the writ drops.

The period of the writ can, by legislation and by instruction to the governor general of Canada, be increased. The tests of endurance and accomplishment can be made more severe.

If the period of the writ were doubled or tripled, all candidates would begin to experience the unease that accompanies the ups and downs of those two tests.

Candidates who hang around Vegas to finish a card game or who stay away from their riding for the entire five weeks of a campaign in order to avoid the financial commitment of being without work would have a much harder time dealing with the negative press if their exposure was months, instead of weeks, long. A five-week campaign takes two weeks to ramp up and one week to sail home. Intense exposure currently happens only during weeks three and four. With only two weeks of exposure, one can get away, metaphorically speaking, with murder.

Lengthening the period of the writ could make quite a difference in many ways. It is impossible to go through the humbling experience of going door to door without learning something about yourself. Questions are asked; answers must be given. If the avoidance must be repeated again and again over a longer period of time, the candidate who avoids meaningful discourse will be exposed for the superficial person he or she is. You can get away with murder for a week or two, but not for months. Over a longer period, rumours fly and media stories begin to circulate. Those who show themselves repeatedly to be inept are much more likely to be revealed.

While the commitment of resources that a politico brings to

an electoral campaign will always be less than the novice, the demand for resources from everyone will grow if the period of the writ is lengthened. A person's ability to hang on to family and friends is harder when a test lasts three months than if it lasts a few weeks. Pizza and cola cost more when more of both is consumed, as they will be if the coterie of dedicated supporters is youthful, excited, and ravenous.

The longer an election campaign goes on, the greater the chance that a candidate's supporting cast will develop tension among its members. Internecine feuds will begin to grow. Campaign managers will have to prove their mettle. Many will quit. For interim periods, the candidates without campaign managers — politicos included — will have no choice but to step in. Leadership can become a serious test even for those who would rather be led and be told what to do.

As tensions grow and as the feuds unfold over the period of a longer campaign, all candidates will begin to feel the isolation that is associated with being the only constant in the mix. Even official agents are known to have quit. They are more likely to do so if revenues and payments must be properly recorded over a time period that is long enough for serious mistakes to be made. Official agents can go to jail for mistakes in the order of only hundreds of dollars. Very few official agents are trained accountants.

The longer the period of the writ becomes, the more daunting it will be for politicos. They mostly got into it for the good luck of winning. There is no downside when your party will reward you one way or another. But if you stand to alienate family and friends because of feuding among them, if the risk rises that money may be received or spent inappropriately, if you are around long enough for slips of the tongue to be held against you before the day of the vote, then running will no longer be an experience that you can dance nimbly through.

For you, the older and more experienced novice, the longer the period of the writ, the better.

You have already survived — for better or worse — the tests of privacy, values, commitment, leadership, and isolation. Your record of achievement prior to your candidacy already demonstrates to interested residents and observers what you are made of. You have already taken a far greater hand in the strategic planning of your campaign than your electoral district association or your party wanted. You know better than most how to implement a strategic plan. The political context within which you must do this if a campaign manager quits — as three did in my case — is no longer strange to you.

For me, the period of the writ, after the first two intense days, was the easiest part of the journey. If the election had gone on for another couple of months, I would have stepped further and further away from the dictates of my party. I would have eschewed, for example, the order to "go after the low-hanging fruit." I would have spent much more time in Vanier, a traditionally Liberal part of my riding. I would have given more of my attention to French-language media coverage of my candidacy. I would have made it increasingly clear that my purpose if elected would be to represent the collective will of my riding to my party and to the government. I would have been empowered to do this because a candidate is legally independent upon being formally recognized by Elections Canada the day after the writ drops.

It is still highly likely, of course, that I would have lost regardless. Novices typically lose. The tests of the gauntlet have become stacked against the novice on many counts in addition to the brevity of electoral campaigns.

After you lose the election, remember that a period something like post-traumatic stress will almost certainly follow. A crescendo begins to build as an election approaches. It builds even more during the election itself and, on the morning that the polls open, you will expect your determination and your pride to take you over the top. Almost everyone who has joined your team will tell you that you are certain to do much better than anyone expects. You prepare for the reward that, in a professional context, goes to those who have planned expertly and done their work diligently. But when you lose, it will all be over, instantly, and only your spouse or partner will be there to help you recover your pride. A former leader of the Liberal Party of Canada wrote an entire book in which he tried to reconcile his damaged ego to its fate after his lost election.

There are so many reasons why "good people" do not go into politics.

If you have been at the precipice for a while and are wondering whether to make the jump, it is unlikely, as my friend the political science professor said, that the contents of this book will make your decision any easier. If you remain poised, however, my advice is "Go ahead. Do it!" Yes, it's true that democracy in Canada is slowly turning on its head. Governance by the many is becoming governance by the few. But the dynamics in our democratic institutions are reflecting parallel dynamics happening everywhere else.

I say "do it" because fail-safe adjustments — such as locking in elements of the gauntlet and extending the period of the writ — can still be made. I may not have hit upon the best solutions. But I am certain that the best solutions will not be conceived of by politicos who are or who aspire to be career politicians.

If people like you and I do not have the courage to step into the electoral process and learn what can be done to secure the power of interested citizens to have meaningful influence over their governors, what hope will there be for our democracy in the long term? Though the damage to us personally and financially may be considerable, the lessons we learn and the lessons we teach will spread wider if we jump than if we do not. I say "do it" because there are a number of important causes we humans can serve in our societies. Running for public office in a democracy is one of the greatest of them.

Immediately after submitting my name for possible nomination by the Conservative Party of Canada as their candidate in the Ontario riding of Ottawa–Vanier, I called the Liberal Party minister I had been executive assistant to thirty years before. I wanted him to know of my intention before it became public. His answer was that, regardless of party affiliation, to run for elected office is ennobling. It really is.

While you may not have the energy to stay with the business of politics after you lose, you will have gained something in the effort that provides grist for stories you will tell again and again, and write about. Your listeners and your readers will know those stories to be important. Democracy is important. You sacrificed something in order to learn what you will have earned the right to talk about and to write about. Jump. And, after you recover, do not keep silent.

ACKNOWLEDGMENTS

To all those who joined me in my venture, whether they went the distance with me or not, I owe a profound "thank you." In each and every case, the willingness of a sitting politician or a volunteer to join with me provided a boost that propelled me much further forward than disappointments between us ever pulled me back. I owe a special debt to the few who still stood with me on the day of the vote, and above all to my wife and my official agent.

This book is like the bounce that follows after an object launched by the catapult first lands.

The bounce would not have happened without the encouragement of an article written by David Reevely in the *Ottawa Citizen* (July 4, 2014) in which he referred readers to my story and observed that people should listen to what defeated candidates have to say. His article followed a piece of my own that had appeared on the website of Samara Canada a month earlier. That was when I first described running for Parliament as something akin to running a gauntlet. By hosting that description on their website, the citizens' advocacy group strengthened my belief that the record of my unsuccessful run could become a bookend to the contents of *Tragedy in the Commons* by Alison Loat and Michael MacMillan.

Carra Simpson, at Page Two Strategic Publishing, received my proposal for this book with enthusiasm. She brought it to the attention of Trena White, one of the principals of the firm, who undertook without reserve to help me steer a course through editing, artwork, and printing. Michelle MacAleese, as editor, challenged me to go beyond the overview and diary that I had thought would be the sum total of what I had to say. With her guidance, my experiences became much more than the detailing of personal angst.

I knew, shortly after being designated as candidate, that I was in trouble. I learned along the way that Canada's electoral process is in trouble as well.

I want to acknowledge the 14,184 residents in Ottawa–Vanier who voted for me in the 2011 federal election, the 53,000 residents in my riding who went to the polls on May 2 in that year, and the 61.1% of Canadian citizens eligible to vote who actually did so. I exhort all of them, and even more the 38.9% of citizens who did not vote, to take politics more seriously between elections. In a healthy democracy, we candidates run for you, the people of Canada. There should be no room for doubt about that.

APPENDIX

READINESS QUIZ FOR NOVICE CANDIDATES

Each question is worded so that a rating of zero means "no" and 10 means a strong "yes".

THE TEST OF PRIVACY

1. Do members of your immediate and extended family already associate you with the political party that you hope to represent?
2. Do your friends and neighbours already associate you with the political party you hope to represent?
3. Will your personal relationships be enhanced by your standing publicly for the political party you have chosen?
4. Will your professional relationships be enhanced by your standing publicly for the political party you have chosen?

THE TEST OF VALUES

1. Are you comfortable saying what your five core values are to the journalist who interviews you or when you stand on a public stage?
2. Are you comfortable saying which of your core values line up most closely with the values associated with the political party you represent?
3. Will you refrain from saying out loud, when asked, which of

the values associated with your party you do not yourself subscribe to?

THE TEST OF COMMITMENT

1. Have you and your partner agreed that you are able to set aside income-earning opportunities throughout the time of your candidacy?
2. When the writ drops, you will be inundated with volunteers, but not before. Are you able to count upon at least ten family members or close friends to provide the help you will need, when you need it, between the time you are nominated to the time that the writ drops?
3. Do you have experience asking for money from family and friends?
4. Are you comfortable with asking associates and strangers for money, in increments of $200 to $1,500?
5. Do you have a track record of bringing associates and strangers together in a pursuit that, in the end, will benefit you — if you are successful — to a far greater extent than it will any of them?

THE TEST OF LEADERSHIP

1. Would you say that you are widely known in your riding for your ability to command and to lead?
2. Are you prepared to give yourself over to the leadership of others even if your reputation for leadership has become at stake?

THE TEST OF ENDURANCE

1. Rites of passage in social or professional settings are a useful way to demonstrate character and prove aptitude.
2. The highs of a personal or professional experience are almost always worth the lows.

3. Quitting a pursuit, once you have committed yourself to it, is never an option.
4. Completing a task in which others around you have a stake and a profound interest can be more important than health itself.

THE TEST OF ISOLATION

1. In your record of achievement to date, have you had to change your network of professional associates along the way?
2. In your record of achievement to date, have you had to change your network of friends along the way?
3. How strong is the interest of your family and friends in being a part of your future in politics?

THE TEST OF ACCOMPLISHMENT

1. Do you agree with the military college slogan "Anything that is worth doing is worth doing well"?
2. When projects you initiated in your professional life were completed, was it important for you to be on hand to close the deals?
3. In the last mile of a marathon, should the runner stick to the game plan?

The maximum score in this quiz, consisting of twenty-four questions, is 240 points. Young politicos and older career politicians, if they are honest with themselves, are likely to score 200 and above. My own rating, had I taken a quiz such as this before my run for public office began, would have been 80 points. A more rational person that I would have declined the opportunity.

www.ingramcontent.com/pod-product-compliance
Ingram Content Group UK Ltd.
Pitfield, Milton Keynes, MK11 3LW, UK
UKHW041305180426
11947UKWH00009B/696